The Integrated Children's System

The Integrated Children's System

Enhancing Social Work and Inter-Agency Practice

Hedy Cleaver, Steve Walker, Jane Scott,
Daniel Cleaver, Wendy Rose,
Harriet Ward and Andy Pithouse

Foreword by Sir Al Aynsley-Green

Jessica Kingsley Publishers
London and Philadelphia

First published in 2008
by Jessica Kingsley Publishers
116 Pentonville Road
London N1 9JB, UK
and
400 Market Street, Suite 400
Philadelphia, PA 19106, USA

www.jkp.com

Library of Congress Cataloging in Publication Data
The integrated children's system : enhancing social work recording and inter-agency practice
/ Hedy Cleaver ... [et al.].
p. cm.
Includes bibliographical references.
ISBN 978-1-84310-944-0 (pb : alk. paper) 1. Social work with children--Great Britain. 2.
Social work administration--Great Britain--Data processing. 3. Information storage and retrieval
systems--Social service. I. Cleaver, Hedy.
HV751.A6I56 2008
362.7--dc22

2008014010

British Library Cataloguing in Publication Data
A CIP catalogue record for this book is available from the British Library

ISBN 978 1 84310 944 0

Printed and bound in Great Britain by
Athenaeum Press, Gateshead, Tyne and Wear

Contents

List of Tables

Foreword

The first piece of research that I commissioned when I came into this post was to find out what young people felt about information sharing. The findings brought home to me the fundamental importance of an honest and open dialogue with vulnerable children in taking these crucial decisions. Get it right and we are well-placed to provide quality services that come together to meet the needs of individual children. Get it wrong and we risk confusing and alienating those we seek to help.

Children tell us clearly what they want when they are experiencing difficulties. First of all they want to talk to someone they can trust. They do not expect miracles but they are looking for respect, honesty and adults who keep their word. They would like to avoid having to tell their story over and over again and they would usually prefer the person they have had contact with to take action on their behalf. They expect that, when problems are serious, information will be shared with professionals in the services that can help them; and they expect to be involved in deciding when this should happen. They understand why a record will be kept about them and their situation but they want to know what has been written about them, who will have access to the information and for what purpose. It is essential, they say, to be kept informed about what is happening at every stage of professionals' involvement and to know what is going to happen next. When action has to be taken, they ask to be fully consulted about decisions and plans that will affect them and members of their families, however hard it is going to be for them. When decisions have been taken they do not want to be forgotten or ignored but, fundamentally, they want someone to know and care how well they are doing.

These utterly straightforward and reasonable requests by children and young people are supported by the UN Convention on the Rights of the Child and by legislation in the United Kingdom. However, they have far-reaching consequences for the way in which those of us in the helping professions carry out our responsibilities and organise our services. They require services to be accessible and responsive according to the circumstances and wishes of children and their families. Processes of gathering information and coming to decisions, planning, taking action and reviewing children's progress, need to be well co-ordinated and as seamless as possible, without unnecessary duplication, bureaucracy or delay. When circumstances become increasingly complex and a child is vulnerable, effective information sharing and planning across agencies is critically important.

It is for these reasons that practitioners need the support of well developed processes for their work and for recording and sharing information. The development of the Integrated Children's System by the Department for Children, Schools and Families aims to provide a more coherent basis for working with children in need and their families, underpinned by a common language and set of principles, and up-to-date access to user-friendly electronic recording. Inevitably, translating such an ambitious initiative from the drawing board into practical reality involves trial and error. This is why the findings of this book are important as they record the experience of four local authorities in England and Wales that piloted the new approach. The book provides valuable learning points for authorities currently involved in the process of implementing the Integrated Children's System.

Sir Al Aynsley-Green
Children's Commissioner for England, at 11 Million

Acknowledgements

Government has a clear ambition to improve outcomes for children so that all children may be able to fulfil their potential. Achieving this requires a formidable programme of change involving every agency working with children and families. The implementation of the Integrated Children's System is an important contribution towards meeting these aims in order to ensure the effective provision of services for children in need. Against this background, a study of four local authorities piloting the new approach early in the development of the Integrated Children's System was bound to be complex. This was further complicated by the composition of the evaluation team being drawn from four universities across England and Wales, and funding being provided by three different government departments in England together with the Welsh Assembly Government. It has been the commitment of many people and their support that has enabled the study of the pilots to be achieved successfully.

We are indebted to the research managers and policy officials in England and Wales who steered the project through from beginning to end. Particular gratitude is owed to Dr Carolyn Davies, Jenny Gray OBE and Helen Jones, in what is now the Department for Children, Schools and Families, and Jonathan Corbett, Assistant Chief Inspector in Wales. The study was throughout a partnership between the evaluation team and the four pilot authorities and their local agencies. We are full of respect for the staff involved who retained a positive outlook through all the challenges each authority faced at one time or another, and who worked enthusiastically with us each step of the way. We would wish to thank all the practitioners and managers who filled in questionnaires and openly shared their views with us at the study workshops. A number of young people looked after also completed questionnaires which gave us insights into their perspectives on how services were working for them. We are enormously grateful to them. In each local authority IT managers and the Integrated Children's System lead officer generously gave us time and helped us to understand their systems. Their contribution has also been greatly valued.

A research advisory group was established from the beginning of the study which scrutinised the methodology and progress of the evaluation from the different perspectives of research, policy and children's service management. We would wish to mark the collective and individual support and advice given by the following: Carolyn Davies (who chaired the advisory group), Charlie Beaumont, Amanda Edwards, Naomi Eisenstadt, Deborah Ghate, Jenny Gray, Eileen Henneberry, Helen Jones, Margaret Lynch, Alan McNamara, Jacqui Moyle, Sara Scott, Ian Sinclair, Stuart Tanner, Caroline Thomas and John Twiddy. This list is not exclusive and we were grateful for professional advice and administrative support from many others.

Chapter 1

Introduction to the Study

The full-scale introduction of new policies and delivery mechanisms should, wherever possible, be preceded by closely monitored pilots. Phased introductions help not only to inform implementation but also to identify and prevent unintended consequences.

(Jowell 2003, p.5)

Introduction

The Integrated Children's System has been designed to ensure that assessment, planning and decision making lead to good outcomes for children in need and their families. The system became fully operational in English local authority children's social care for all the core processes undertaken by them for children in need on 1 January 2007, and on 31 December 2006 in Wales. The Government is committed to the development of the Integrated Children's System and to its implementation nationally in England and Wales as part of its major reform programme to improve outcomes for all children. This was first signalled publicly in England and Wales in 2000 (Cm 4776 2000).

At an early point during the development phase, it was recognised that an integrated approach to the assessment and delivery of services to children in need and their families would have a far reaching impact on local children's social care and their partner agencies. It would, therefore, be essential for a number of local authorities to pilot the Integrated Children's System to contribute to the process of its development. Furthermore, the findings would be important in informing local children's social care throughout England and Wales in preparation for national implementation.

Funding for such a study was provided in 2002 by the Treasury through its Evidence Based Policy Fund with matched funding provided since then by the Department of Health, the Welsh Assembly Government and the then Department for Education and Skills (now the Department for Children, Schools and Families). This enabled the system to be piloted in four authorities across England and Wales. The research evaluating the impact of the Integrated Children's System has been undertaken by an inter-university team led by Royal Holloway, University of London.

The Integrated Children's System in the current policy context

The Integrated Children's System has been under development since 2000 during which time there have been major developments in the policy and organisational context of children's services as part of the Government's commitment to improving the wellbeing of all children. This first section examines the policy context and the role of the Integrated Children's System in the Government's agenda.

The Integrated Children's System is a key strand in the Government's overall change agenda for children's services as set out in England in the Green Paper, Every Child Matters (Cm 5860 2003) and in Wales in Children and Young People: Rights to Action (Welsh Assembly Government 2004) and in the subsequent legislation, the Children Act 2004. Both Every Child Matters and Children and Young People: Rights to Action are conceived as whole-system reform programmes. There are a number of critical features about these programmes to which current developments, including the Integrated Children's System, are making an important contribution:

- definition of what is meant by good outcomes for children that are agreed by children and their families as well as by professionals and that will be used to measure children's progress

- recognition that there is an important relationship between different areas of a child's life, such as educational achievement and feeling safe from harm, and that therefore children's outcomes are inter-dependent

- acknowledgement that early identification of additional needs is required if a child faces obstacles in fulfilling his or her potential, to ensure that appropriate help and support can be provided at the time it is required

- emphasis on sharing information with children and families in order to work in partnership with them

- emphasis on sharing relevant information between universal services and other agencies in contact with a child when there are concerns in order to build up a comprehensive picture of what is happening

- improvement in the delivery of services to children and families, requiring reconfiguration of the services around the child and family, and integration of services at the point of delivery and in management and commissioning

- development of electronic systems to improve the efficiency and effectiveness of record keeping and information sharing in ʿ pport of good professional practice and management

- evaluation of how well children are doing both on an individual basis and also on a wider population basis, to inform practice, management and policy

- a well trained, competent and confident workforce to work with children and families, including those able to provide specialised help when needed.

Developing an outcomes-based approach to children and families: policy for children looked after

Successive governments have placed increasing emphasis on improving outcomes for children over the last two decades, starting with those children considered to be most vulnerable and with the poorest outcomes. This approach has become more explicit and has been extended to embrace all children through the publication of the policies outlined in Every Child Matters (Cm 5860 2003) and Children and Young People: Rights to Action (Welsh Assembly Government 2004).

The first group of children for whom the importance of outcomes were identified were those defined as children in need under the Children Act 1989 (although the concept of outcomes was implied rather than explicit at that time). Local authorities were given a clear duty in the legislation 'to safe-guard and promote the welfare of children within their area who are in need … by providing a range and level of services appropriate to their needs' (Children Act 1989, s17 (1)). Children in need were defined as those children 'unlikely to achieve, or maintain, or to have the opportunity of achieving or maintaining, a reasonable standard of health or development without the pro-vision for him of services by a local authority…' (s17 (10)). The emphasis was, therefore, on identifying those children and addressing their developmental needs.

The children in need who were considered especially vulnerable at this stage were children looked after away from home and for whom the local authority assumed a degree of parental responsibility. Concern focused on these children because serious doubts were being expressed about the success of their experiences of growing up in residential and foster care. This led to the development of the Looking After Children: Good Parenting, Good Outcomes programme, introduced by the Department of Health in 1995 (Department of Health 1995a). Seven dimensions of children's developmental needs were considered to be critical to achieving satisfactory outcomes for children looked after, which required careful assessment and review by those responsible for their upbringing (Parker *et al.* 1991; Ward 1995a). The programme included a series of age-related schedules across the seven dimensions and other materials to be used to assess, record and review children's progress, and ensure appropriate action was taken.

Subsequently, improving the outcomes and life chances for looked after children became an integral part of major government programmes in both England and Wales. Quality Protects in England and Children First in Wales were outlined in the UK and Welsh Assembly Government's Objectives for Children's Social Services in England and Wales (Department of Health 1999; Welsh Office 1999). As a result, two new routine collections of information were introduced by the Department of Health and the National Assembly for Wales, the first on outcomes for children looked after and the second on care leavers, in order to monitor the progress being made by local authorities in meeting the government objectives for this group of children.

Since then, attention has continued to be directed towards improving the outcomes of children looked after through new legislation and other policy initiatives, including:

- the Children (Leaving Care) Act 2000 and the introduction of personal advisers and Pathway Plans
- the Adoption and Children Act 2002 and its emphasis on greater security and permanence
- promoting the educational achievement and health of looked after children (Department of Health 2002a; HM Government 2006a; National Assembly for Wales 2001a, 2006; Social Exclusion Unit 2003)
- National Service Framework for Children, Young People and Maternity Services (Department of Health and Department for Education and Skills 2004; National Assembly for Wales 2005)

which sets out national standards for health and social care for children, considering particularly the needs of children and young people looked after.

Refocusing children's services on children in need and the development of the Assessment Framework

While the Looking After Children: Good Parenting, Good Outcomes programme (Department of Health 1995a) was being implemented, research and inspection findings were providing worrying information about the extent to which children and their families, where there were unmet needs, were being increasingly referred to local child protection processes and then filtered out when they might have benefited from family support or other services (Department of Health 1995b; Social Services Inspectorate 1997). Some professionals believed that the only way to obtain priority from social services for children about whom there were concerns was to identify their difficulties in terms of risk of harm. Services to support families in the community, however, were not being made available at an early enough stage either because their needs were inadequately identified or because an appropriate range of services had not been planned and developed. The Government response in 1996 was to promote a new strategy for refocusing children's services so that they would become more broadly based, underpinned by the principle that services should be needs led. It was announced that good assessment was the key to achieving the required change and that all social services should have procedures for assessing the need for services of the children and families referred to them (Armstrong 1997).

The Labour Government on coming to power in 1997 identified the importance of assessment as a critical part of its commitment to promoting the welfare of all children. As a result one of the key objectives for children's social services was 'to ensure that referral and assessment processes discriminate effectively between different types and levels of need and produce a timely service response' (Department of Health 1999, p.20; see also Welsh Office 1999, Circular 20/99). A conceptual framework for understanding what was happening to children in need within the context of their families and the wider community where they lived was developed, to be used in a structured and systematic way to gather information, analyse and record it, as the foundation for effective planning and intervention.

Guidance on the new Assessment Framework was issued jointly in England in 2000 by the Department of Health, Department for Education and Employment and the Home Office, and in Wales by the National Assembly for Wales, signalling the corporate responsibility of public authorities for children in need (Department of Health *et al.* 2000a; National Assembly for Wales 2001b). This marked the beginning of a more coherent cross-government approach to assessing children's needs, a problem which had featured prominently at national as well as local level since the birth of the welfare state and the Children Act 1948. As Kellmer Pringle and Naidoo (1975) observed over 30 years ago:

> Although the Department of Health and Social Security has overall responsibility for assessment, under the 1944 Education Act, local education authorities have a duty to examine children from the age of two where a handicap is suspected. Also, in 1968, the Home Office in the White Paper, 'Children in Trouble', recognized a need to develop facilities for the observation and assessment of social handicap as a way of supporting families and dealing with juvenile delinquents. Thus there are, in effect, three government departments concerned with assessment and this often creates obstacles to communication about individuals and to the coordination of available services.
>
> (Kellmer Pringle and Naidoo 1975, p.57)

Practice guidance which accompanied the Assessment Framework (Department of Health 2000; National Assembly for Wales 2001b) emphasised the importance of developing knowledge about children whose needs were sometimes overlooked or not fully understood or who perhaps were primarily the responsibility of a different statutory service, such as children from asylum seeking families, children who were young carers, disabled children, or children from black and ethnic minority families. The significance of the Guidance was strengthened by its being issued under section 7 of the Local Authority Social Services Act 1970 and the Assessment Framework was incorporated into a range of other government guidance relating to children and families, including the then new edition of Working Together to Safeguard Children (Department of Health, Home Office and Department for Education and Employment 1999; National Assembly for Wales 2000a).

Also accompanying the Guidance was a set of records for referral and essential information, initial assessments and core assessments (the latter divided into five age bands). The structure of each core assessment record was the same, information gathering followed by analysis and planning (Department of Health and Cleaver 2000). Implementation of the Assessment Framework was undertaken in England for completion by the end of March 2001 and begun in Wales in 2001.

Improving outcomes for all children: Every Child Matters, Children and Young People: Rights to Action and the Common Assessment Framework

In order to address its wider aspirations for all children, the UK Government established the Children and Young People's Unit in 2000, a high profile unit within government with the task of developing an overarching strategy for children's services in England. The Unit launched its work for and with children and young people by consulting on an outcomes framework, reflecting the UK Government's ambitions for children and encompassing all aspects of their lives (Children and Young People's Unit 2001). These outcomes were consolidated in the Green Paper, Every Child Matters (Cm 5860 2003):

- being healthy
- staying safe
- enjoying and achieving
- making a positive contribution
- achieving economic wellbeing.

In November 2000, the National Assembly for Wales published Children and Young People: A Framework for Partnership. That policy document began with a commitment to the United Nations Convention on the Rights of the Child. The Convention sets out how the Assembly Government should act in all dealings with children and young people. Framework for Partnership also proposed a new method of planning services for children and young people through partnerships of local authorities, the health service, and other local bodies (National Assembly for Wales 2000b). It promised a simpler way of paying grants to local authorities. It set out a commitment to listening to children and young people, and referred to plans to establish a Children's Commissioner for Wales.

The Children's Commissioner was appointed in Wales in 2001 with powers to review the effect of policies on, and the delivery of services to, children and young people. He can consider anything affecting them, based on their views. To ensure that policy development was informed by the views of children and young people, the Assembly Government supported the development of a national organisation to represent the views of children and young people.

The views of the Children's Commissioner and children and young people themselves informed the commitment to children in Wales set out in Children and Young People: Rights to Action (Welsh Assembly Government 2004). Rights to Action set out the Assembly Government's aspirations for children and young people in Wales to:

- have a flying start in life
- have a comprehensive range of education and learning opportunities
- enjoy the best possible health and are free from abuse, victimisation and exploitation
- have access to play, leisure, sporting and cultural activities
- ensure they are listened to, treated with respect, and have their race and cultural identity recognised
- have a safe home and a community which supports physical and emotional wellbeing
- ensure they are not disadvantaged by poverty.

These outcomes, as identified in England and Wales, have now been embedded in the Children Act 2004, and have created a challenging and far-reaching programme of children's services reform.

Within these reforms there is a strong commitment to early intervention and effective protection, which has led to the question of how children with additional needs can be identified earlier and appropriate help provided. As a result, in England a Common Assessment Framework (HM Government 2006b) has been developed which is a process for undertaking early assessments of children. A similar framework is currently under development in Wales. Both are based on the conceptual framework of the Framework for the Assessment of Children in Need and their Families, and can be used across services for all children. In England the process is supported by a simple pre-assessment checklist and a single assessment record. The Common Assessment Framework aims to:

- provide a common language and understanding of children's needs for all practitioners working with children and families
- ensure appropriate referral if a more specialist service is required and that core information follows the child to reduce duplication

- ensure that evidence is consistently recorded to high, credible standards
- enable practitioners to work together and share information more effectively
- facilitate the delivery to children and families of effective and timely universal services and any additional services.

The Common Assessment Framework has been implemented across England from April 2006, with the aim of being fully embedded by March 2008.

Information sharing and multi-agency working

Throughout the development of the children's services reform agenda, there has been a strong and prevailing theme about the importance of improving information sharing both within agencies and between all those who work with children and young people, in whatever sector or capacity. There have been clear statements from Government that good information sharing is seen as the key to successful collaborative working across children's services to improve the outcomes for children and young people. This has been rein-forced by the findings from safeguarding children inquiries discussed below. Consequently, a 'Duty to Co-operate' has been incorporated into the Children Act 2004, s10, which requires local action to improve information sharing and to address some of the systemic and cultural barriers that exist. The Government has now issued for the first time cross-government guidance in England on information sharing (HM Government 2006c; 2006d) which addresses the sensitive issues of consent, confidentiality, professional judge-ment and good practice, set within the context of current legislation. In Wales the Wales Accord for the Sharing of Personal Information (Welsh Assembly Government 2006) has been developed. This sets out a framework for intelli-gent information sharing in health and social care.

A further development to enable practitioners to contact each other easily, to share relevant information and prevent duplication and delay, is the estab-lishment of ContactPoint (previously known by the working title of the Infor-mation Sharing Index). ContactPoint will be an online directory available to authorised staff in England to find out who else is working with the same child. It will contain basic information about a child, parents or carers, and the services and professionals involved, but no detailed information nor any case data. Access will be restricted to authorised users who need it as part of their work. There have been a number of authorities which have been trailblazers for this approach (Cleaver *et al.* 2004a) and they have demonstrated that there are some important benefits from using this type of tool. The intention is to make ContactPoint available to local authorities in England during 2008. In Wales work is under way to evaluate the cost and benefits for children in Wales of implementing such an approach.

At the same time as attention has been given to improving information sharing, there has been equal policy emphasis on the promotion of integrated services and multi-agency working. This is argued on the grounds of effectiveness in addressing the wide range of cross-cutting risk factors that contribute to poor outcomes for children and young people. A diversity of models for multi-agency working is being encouraged in England and Wales through a range of different services, including in England Children's Trusts, and Sure Start Children's Centres, and in Wales Children and Young People's Framework Partnerships and Flying Start, and likely to be the subject of further government guidance.

Electronic care records

As part of its modernising agenda, the UK Government laid out its intentions for the development of e-government with a cross-government strategy for the public services (Cabinet Office 2000). This has required the introduction of electronic social care records in children's social care by 2005, thereby ensuring information can be collected, held and transmitted to improve the efficient delivery of services to children and families. The contribution of the Integrated Children's System to achieving these requirements was reinforced in the Local Authority Circular on Transforming Children's Services (LAC(2002)19, 19 December 2002) which restated the Government's objectives for children's social services:

> Objective 11: Enhancing the development and use of management information systems; improving quality assurance systems to ensure that services are delivered according to requirements and are meeting local and national objectives; and developing financial management strategies.

In this circular, local authorities were advised to pay attention to how information systems were designed and used to help control for procedural and practice compliance, and which would then be able to underpin quality assurance. The Integrated Children's System records were identified as constituting a major element of the electronic case record and, at the same time, would collect information on children in need and their families as part of the Children's Social Services Core Information Requirements.

Findings from safeguarding children inquiries

The development of the Integrated Children's System has been informed throughout by findings from research, inspection and inquiries. There were two particularly significant inquiries about policy and practice in relation to safeguarding children, which reported during the period of the study of the pilots and have had far-reaching influence on national policy. The first was the Victoria Climbié Inquiry, conducted by Lord Laming, which reported in 2003 (Cm 5730 2003), and the second concerned the safeguarding of children from sexual offenders following the conviction of Ian Huntley for the murder of two children, conducted by Sir Michael Bichard (HC 653 2004). The Victoria Climbié Inquiry identified some fundamental problems in the safeguarding system, including the gathering, storing and sharing of information between agencies. The Bichard Inquiry also drew attention to the need for more effective intra- and inter-agency information sharing: 'because both [police and social services] viewed each case in isolation and because social services failed to share information effectively with the police' (HC 653 2004, para.8, p.2).

In the Government's response to the Victoria Climbié Inquiry Report (Cm 5861 2003), it acknowledged the problems located in the safeguarding system but affirmed that with regard to information sharing some aspects of these problems were being addressed by the development of the Integrated Children's System:

> The Integrated Children System has been designed to enable local organisations to work together, share information more easily and facilitate referrals between organisations. It will benefit children and families by enabling them to understand what information organisations are asking for and why, and will help them judge whether they are getting the help they need. (Cm 5861 2003, para.61, p.14)

Government continues to affirm the importance it attaches to the implementation of the Integrated Children's System by local authorities as an integral part of their responsibility to drive improvements in frontline practice and increase the safety of children and young people in their area (HM Government 2007).

Effective implementation of new policy

Experience of implementing recent policy changes in children's services has been increasingly well documented through the evaluation of trailblazers or pathfinders (see, for example, Cleaver *et al.* 2004a, in relation to developing

Information Sharing and Assessment Systems, and Brandon *et al.* 2006, in relation to the early implementers of the Common Assessment Framework). There have also been a number of research studies which have explored the implementation of new policy directives into practice (see, for example, Jones *et al.* 1998 and Ward 1995a, in relation to the Looking After Children materials, and Cleaver *et al.* 2004b, and Rose, Aldgate and Barnes 2007, in relation to the Assessment Framework). The lessons learned from these studies about what promotes effective implementation and what may become barriers have been built into the design and development of later policy initiatives and into the guidance in preparation for implementation (see Corrick, Jones and Ward 1995; Department of Health *et al.* 2000a).

The implementation of the current policy agenda of Every Child Matters and Children and Young People: Rights to Action has been described as an essentially rational model which 'starts with interagency governance at a national level, moves down through an integrated strategy and processes, to the front line where delivery of services takes place through the efforts of social care, education and health specialists' (Hudson 2005, p.31). Hudson goes on to argue that such a model requires attention to be addressed to all levels simultaneously, and that 'failure at any one level could undermine the chances of achieving the desired outcomes' (*ibid.*). This is a point which is underlined in many of the studies cited above and in other reports (see, for example, the stakeholder report of the Inter-Agency Group, *From Vision to Reality: Transforming Outcomes for Children and Families,* 2004). It was also clearly exemplified in a case study of implementing the Assessment Framework, which revealed the complex reality for service organisations involved in delivering change (Rose *et al.* 2007).

The children's workforce

The challenges involved in implementing new policy initiatives have highlighted issues about the current state of the children's services workforce. Concerns have been expressed and debated about the impact on workforce development of the policy agenda with its programme of far-reaching change. Gupta and Blewett (2007) argue with others that recognition has to be given to the chronic problems of recruiting and retaining workers in a range of child care settings and ensuring that practitioners are trained, managed and supported to be able to carry out skilled direct work with children and families. They suggest there is a need for cultural as well as structural change in order to reduce the bureaucratic load on practitioners and to enhance the capacity and quality of the workforce delivering services (Gupta and Blewett 2007). These are matters currently being addressed through the prospectus of the Common Core of Skills and Knowledge required for the children's workforce (HM Government 2005a) and the Children's Workforce Strategy (HM Government 2005b). They have been important considerations in the development of the Integrated Children's System.

The development of the Integrated Children's System

This chapter has outlined some of the contextual factors which have influenced the development of the Integrated Children's System. It has been launched in a very different and more complex policy context from that of its conception when the objectives were more limited, essentially to bringing coherence to the processes of work with children in need and their families. The Integrated Children's System is now a critical element of both the Every Child Matters and Children and Young People: Rights to Action major reform programmes, which emphasise improving outcomes for all children by early identification of need, information sharing and multi-agency working by practitioners, and effective delivery of services, underpinned by a competent and confident workforce and efficient information management systems. This section describes the Integrated Children's System and introduces the study evaluating the piloting of the system.

The Government announced the development of the Integrated Children's System in 2000 in its response to the inquiry report into the abuse of children in care in North Wales, Learning the Lessons (Cm 4776 2000).

> When the Assessment Framework is implemented, children and young people who start to be looked after will have had a core assessment which will provide baseline information about their needs to ensure appropriate placement matching and care planning. The Assessment Framework is being integrated with the Looking After Children materials to produce an Integrated Children's System. This will provide an assessment planning intervention and reviewing model for all children in need. (Cm 4776 2000, p.42)

The development of the Integrated Children's System represents not only a way of joining up the previous developments of the Looking After Children materials (Department of Health 1995c) and the Framework for the Assessment for Children in Need and their Families (Department of Health et al. 2000a; National Assembly for Wales 2001b) to include work with all children in need but also builds on those developments both conceptually and in terms of the lessons learned from implementation. Part of the rationale for the development has been to address concerns about poor decision making and planning for children in need (especially those children looked after) and to improve poor recording, graphically highlighted in inspections (Social Services Inspectorate 1998). The use of the word 'integrated' in the title conveys the integration of the processes of working with children in need from first contact through to the point of final review of the child's plan and intervention ceases.

The system is comprised of three elements:

- a framework for assessment, planning, intervention and reviewing, providing a single and coherent approach for undertaking these key processes of working with children in need

- a set of data requirements for children's services in relation to children in need and their families; these data contribute both to individual case planning and to the overall information required to plan and deliver children's services

- exemplars of case records for use by children's services practitioners to assist local authorities in developing their e-social care records for children and the IT system to support the implementation of the Integrated Children's System.

The conceptual framework is based on a set of underpinning principles, outlined in the box opposite. They acknowledge not only the importance of adopting a developmental/ecological approach in assessment and planning but also that a holistic view of a child and family's wellbeing will involve professionals from the universal services already known to a family, as well as other services. In this sense, the Integrated Children's System was perceived as strengthening integrated practice between the statutory and voluntary sector services for children in need, through the use of a common language about children's needs and the influences on their development, and improved communication and information sharing between practitioners.

Underlying a coherent approach to the processes of working with children in need and their families, and fundamental to the design of the Integrated Children's System, is a commitment to a common approach to the delivery and recording of those key processes, supported by good information technology. The Integrated Children's System is not itself an IT system but has been designed to be implemented as an electronic system and, therefore,

PRINCIPLES UNDERPINNING THE INTEGRATED CHILDREN SYSTEM

Every process:

- is child centred
- is rooted in child development
- is ecological in its approach
- ensures equality of opportunity
- involves working with children and families
- builds on strengths as well as identifies difficulties
- is inter-agency in its approach
- is a continuing process, not a single event
- involves assessment carried out in parallel with other actions and providing services
- is grounded in evidence-based knowledge.

requires the development of an appropriate IT system in each local authority. In consequence, the Department of Health and later the Department for Education and Skills issued a set of Core Data Requirements, outlining the information to be collected and processed for children in need, for use in commissioning local authority IT systems (Department for Education and Skills 2003a).

The case records constitute a critical element in the Integrated Children's System as the basis for direct work with children in need and their families and for the collection of aggregated data for service planning and commissioning. Furthermore, the records have been perceived as playing an important part in improving information sharing (Department for Education and Skills 2006a). The development of ContactPoint will require records to be accurate and electronically available to provide information about which agencies are providing services to children and families. Twenty-six exemplars of case records have been developed and issued to encompass the circumstances in which information may be required to be recorded for children in need. These are being updated and added to in response to changes in legislation and government guidance.

A high level of communication between the Department of Health (and subsequently the Department for Education and Skills, now the Department for Children, Schools and Families), the National Assembly for Wales and local authority children's social care has been maintained throughout the development of the Integrated Children's System, to seek the views of key stakeholders and to inform those who would have responsibility for implementing the new system. Briefing Papers (Department of Health and Department for Education and Skills 2000–2005) were issued from November 2000. In addition, exemplars of the records, an electronic demonstrator (Department for Education and Skills 2003b) and other materials were issued to local authorities, a national consultation exercise was held in 2002, and regional conferences were held on an annual basis in England and Wales during this period. It was recognised that the widest possible engagement with the field was necessary from the start of the project, particularly to ensure that the contribution of the Integrated Children's System to the overall change agenda for children was understood. Careful consideration was given to issues of implementation and the importance of piloting the system was identified during the early stages of its development. This study was, therefore, incorporated into the national development plan with the aim of evaluating the implementation of different dimensions of the system in four pilots by authorities in England and Wales.

Piloting the Integrated Children's System: an introduction to the study

An important innovation in recent years has been the phased introduction of major government policies or programmes, allowing them to be tested, evaluated and adjusted where necessary, before being rolled out nationally.

(Jowell 2003, p.3)

As a result of the development work thus far, in November 2001 a research proposal to evaluate an integrated system for the delivery of services for children in need and their families was put to the Treasury's Evidence Based Policy Fund, which at the time was inviting bids for the third tranche of the Fund. This fund had been launched in response to the Cabinet Office report, Adding It Up (Performance and Innovation Unit 2000). The report had recommended 'more and better use of pilots to test the impacts of policies before national roll-out' (p.6).

The Evidence Based Policy Fund was conceived as a seed corn fund to promote the supply of research and analysis for cross-cutting policy. It was also seen as a means of strengthening links between universities, research institutes and Government through the financing of applied research on some of the Government's priority topics. Over £2 million had already been committed to almost 30 research projects and a further £1.9 million was being made available to advance the Government's commitment to policy-making based on sound evidence.

Proposals were being sought for research in areas which spanned the conventional departmental boundaries and which were, therefore, unlikely to come within normal departmental funding schemes. Selection criteria were defined in terms of: policy relevance; additionality, including why the research was of inter-agency relevance; methodology; feasibility; and value for money. Funding was on the basis of the Evidence Based Policy Fund providing 50 per cent of project costs, with sponsoring departments providing matching funds, and this could be extended over more than one financial year.

An application for funding was made by an unusual inter-university collaboration across English and Welsh universities, led by Royal Holloway, University of London, and including Loughborough University, the Open University and the University of Wales, Cardiff. It was unusual in two respects. First, such collaborations across so many university research departments are rare and require a high level of skilful management and co-ordination to work effectively. Second, most of the members of the team had previously been involved either in the development of the Looking After Children materials, or in the Framework for the Assessment of Children in Need and their Families and, subsequently, the Integrated Children's System. This increased their commitment to finding out how the new approach would work in practice and whether it would assist in improving practice in the way envisaged in the design. The team worked hard to ensure that its prior involvement would not bias the rigour of its evaluation and built in external scrutiny throughout with the use of a research advisory group drawn from Government, academics and local authorities.

The research study through the four pilots in England and Wales set out to explore whether the Integrated Children's System:

- improves the quality of direct work with children and families
- provides the foundation for achieving better outcomes for children and young people

- supports inter-agency working and facilitates information sharing
- provides the information needed to support planning processes at both individual and strategic levels
- assists the use and development of performance management.

Another set of aims related to the authorities' IT systems. The research study would explore the relationship between the implementation of the Integrated Children's System and the development of electronic systems in the pilot authorities, by asking:

- how much the Integrated Children's System IT implementation has had an impact on a pilot authority's overall IT plans
- what is the functionality of the IT systems developed to support the Integrated Children's System
- what are the different approaches taken by the pilot authorities in the development and implementation of IT systems to support the Integrated Children's System (including ascertaining what has worked well and what has been more difficult).

In this respect, piloting the Integrated Children's System has combined an opportunity to study both impact and process (Jowell 2003) and in particular to identify 'enablers' and 'blockers' in implementing the system (Inter-Agency Group 2004). This is vitally important because the system involves significant changes in culture and practice in children's services, the challenge of developing and using electronic systems for record keeping and information management, and there are major expectations about the improvements it will bring in information sharing between agencies. Ultimately, the test of its success will be whether it lays the foundation for improving outcomes for children in need and their families as a result of children's services interventions.

The report is structured in two parts. The book examines the findings of the study in relation to the process and impact of implementing the Integrated Children's System from the perspective of managers, practitioners and some of the children looked after. It considers the impact on practice and on inter-agency working. Finally, it discusses the pilot authorities' experience of developing electronic systems to support their implementation of the Integrated Children's System and the issues which have emerged.

The use of language and terminology requires great care to ensure accuracy, shared understanding and respect. During the development of the

Integrated Children's System and the completion of this study, between 2000 and 2006, the major changes already outlined in policy, legislation and organisational arrangements resulted in new terminology to describe statutory children's services in England. Social services departments no longer exist and the primary elements for the new arrangements in local authorities for children's services are education and children's social care. Wales on the other hand, under the provisions of the Children Act 2004, continues to deliver social services to adults and children through a single local authority structure with a Director of Social Services. In order to avoid unnecessary clumsiness, where there are general references to statutory child welfare services in England and Wales in the report, they are referred to as children's social care. It is hoped that Welsh readers of the report will not take this as a lack of respect but an acknowledgement of the important differences developing between Wales and England.

Chapter 2

Implementing the Integrated Children's System

Introduction

This chapter explores the implementation of the Integrated Children's System and is in three parts. The first considers the nature and scope of the change required by the pilot authorities to implement the Integrated Children's System, while the second and third identify the approach they took to implementation. To explore these issues information has been drawn from the following sources:

- formal interviews with the link officer in each authority
- feedback from practitioners and managers during training sessions provided by the research team in each authority
- messages and insights provided by managers and practitioners attending a series of research-led project conferences
- feedback and presentations given by the pilot authorities at regional conferences.

Nature and scope of the change

The likelihood that an organisation will successfully implement change is dependent upon two main factors: the characteristics of the organisation – size, systems, structure, staff and culture – and the nature of the change (Docherty and Horne 2002).

Organisational characteristics

Four pilot authorities were involved in the study: a Shire County, a London Borough, a Welsh Local Authority and a Unitary Authority. The following brief description of these authorities reveals considerable differences in relation to their size and structure.

SIZE AND STRUCTURE

The participating **Shire County** is one of England's largest shire counties, serving a diverse mix of urban and rural communities with a population of 1,140,700 (1991 Census data). Approximately 20 per cent of this population (231,000) were estimated to be between the ages of 0 and 15 years, a proportion consistent with the English average.

The council is predominately white but there are significant black and ethnic minority populations, mainly from Indian, Pakistani and African-Caribbean descent, concentrated in the east of the authority. The 1991 Census estimated that 3.5 per cent of the county's population came from black or ethnic communities.

The east of the county also contains significant pockets of economic and social deprivation and relatively high levels of unemployment, with three wards being ranked the 46th, 50th and 51st most deprived districts in England out of a total of 354 (Department for the Environment, Transport and the Regions 2000).

The council area is covered by four Health Authorities and served by 11 NHS Trusts and 12 Primary Care Groups.

Children's social care experienced its last re-organisation in 2001. The purpose of the re-organisation was to strengthen the department's management structure. The new structure had four area managers who were responsible for fieldwork services, including initial assessment, within a geographical area. There were County Managers for Residential and Leaving Care Services, for the Adoption and Fostering Service and for Quality and Review Services.

Children's social care reported at the time of the research that there were few locum managers employed within the authority, 'maybe one or two', the department was operating with around a 20 per cent vacancy rate, approximately 5 per cent of which were filled by locum staff.

The London Borough is an outer borough with a population of 172,335, with children and young people under the age of 19 years accounting for 22.4 per cent.

People from ethnic minority backgrounds formed 12 per cent of the council's population, including 3 per cent from Irish descent. Of the 9 per cent of the population from black and ethnic minority backgrounds, practically half were of Asian descent.

In relation to economic and social deprivation the council ranks 341 out of 354 authorities (Department for the Environment, Transport and the Regions 2000), making it the lowest ranked London authority.

The authority relates to one NHS Mental Health Trust and one Primary Care Trust.

Children's social care was last re-organised in 2001. The re-organisation took place to meet the requirements of new legislation and guidance, specifically the Children (Leaving Care) Act 2000 Regulations and Guidance (Department of Health 2001a) and the Framework for the Assessment of Children in Need and their Families (Department of Health *et al.* 2000a). This resulted in the local authority introducing a service for children and young people who are looked after and those leaving care and the creation of a specialist initial response team.

At the time of the study children's social care in this local authority was organised into the following specialist service areas:

- Assessment and Family Support
- Looked After and Leaving Care Services
- a discrete service for disabled children
- two locally based Family Support Centres.

At the point of information gathering, 2 out of 14 manager posts were vacant and filled by locum or temporary staff. Among practitioners the vacancy rate was between 10 and 15 per cent. Only a small percentage of these posts were filled by locum staff because strong competition between London Boroughs resulted in acute difficulties in recruitment.

The Welsh Local Authority was established in 1996 following local government re-organisation. It serves a population of approximately 134,500 people, of which 19.6 per cent are aged less than 16 years (a proportion just below the Welsh average). The population consists of 98.9 per cent white British people. Eighteen per cent of its inhabitants speak Welsh.

The main centres of population are in the south and have good access to facilities. However, the authority also serves a number of rural valleys containing scattered communities which experience more difficulties in communication and transport and higher rates of social and health needs.

The Welsh Index of Multiple Deprivation (2000) shows that the authority has three of its wards in the first 20 of the most disadvantaged wards in Wales. Registered unemployment levels in the council are above the Welsh average.

The context for multi-disciplinary work in the local authority is relatively complex considering its size. The authority has to relate to two NHS Trusts: one in relation to community health services (such as community nursing, nutrition and dietetics, occupational therapy, physiotherapy, podiatry and speech and language therapy) and the other for paediatric health and child and adolescent mental health services – the services most commonly used by children receiving a service from children's social services. The authority relates to one Local Health Board.

Children's social services are structured around six service areas:

- children's accommodation
- child disability, assessment, planning and family support
- child protection coordination, emergency duty term and conferences
- partnership, planning, commissioning and development
- looked after children, leaving care and adoption services
- administration.

Each service area is managed by a principal manager. At the time the research was conducted the children's social services was fully staffed.

The Unitary Authority is a small English city which became a unitary authority on 1 April 1996 as part of local government re-organisation. The authority serves a population of 181,091, of which 41,720 are aged less than 19 years, and 2.2 per cent belong to black and ethnic minority groups. The two largest ethnic minority groups in the authority are travelling families and those belonging to the Chinese community.

Approximately 75 per cent of people live inside the city's urban area with the remaining 25 per cent living in small townships and villages where the population density is lower.

The city is relatively prosperous and ranks 219 most deprived out of 354 on the 2000 Indices of Deprivation (Department for the Environment, Transport and the Regions 2000).

Children's social care underwent some restructuring in October 2001, at which point the pilot use of a Referral and Assessment team was made permanent and a Pathway team for care leavers was established. Services were split on the basis of children's age: those aged 0–10 years and those aged 11 years and older. The children's services division also had a discrete Quality Assurance team. Services were provided through: three office bases where social work teams were located; three locally based family centres; and three residential care units (one of which provided short-term breaks for looked after children).

At the time the research was conducted all management posts within children's social care were filled with permanent staff and the small number of social work vacancies in the department, less than 10 per cent, was being covered by locum staff.

STAFF AND CULTURE

Although there were differences in size and structure across the pilot authorities, the literature on organisations and organisational change suggests that the pilot authorities had a similar organisational profile and culture. All the pilot authorities were public service organisations: 'Public Service organisations have a relationship with the users of their services which is quite different from the relationship between a factory and its customers' (Docherty and Horne 2002, p.3). Such organisations emphasise the centrality of formal administrative systems and professional standards of practice. Well-defined policies and procedures and clear mechanisms for decision making and accountability are considered imperative in generating quality of service and eliciting public confidence (see Buchanan and Boddy 1995; Handy 1995, p.23). However, it is in the nature of large formal organisations that they optimise performance within a reasonably predictable environment, hence any major changes are likely to be viewed with some apprehension if not resistance in some quarters (see Brookes and Bates 1994; Docherty and Horne 2002; McConkey 1993). This suggests that in terms of organisational systems and culture the pilot authorities were likely to find the implementation of the Integrated Children's System, which would impact on practitioners and managers at all levels across children's social care, particularly challenging.

Nature of the change

In understanding the scale and nature of change brought about by the Integrated Children's System it is important to remember that the scheme was designed to 'provide an assessment, planning, intervention and reviewing model for all children in need under the Children Act 1989' (Department of Health and Department for Education and Skills 2000–2005, Briefing Paper No.1, p.1). It does not introduce any new legislation, guidance, regulations or timescales. Nor does it introduce a new conceptual framework. Rather it brings together and rationalises the Assessment Framework and Looking After Children system, 'so that the dimensions in the Assessment Framework will be common to work with all children in need and their families' (*ibid.*). It could be argued that the key change introduced by the Integrated Children's System is the expectation that practitioners will enter the information gathered for the key processes of assessment, planning, intervention and review, 'directly into a computerised system with software and visual displays designed to assist them in the organisation of the material' (*ibid.*).

In grasping the impact of the new scheme it is useful to note the observations of Cleaver *et al.* (2004a) who argue that any assessment of the level of change required to implement a new procedure or policy should also consider the amount of change at the level of practice. Thus, the extent of the change required should be evaluated based not on what should be happening but on what is, or was, actually happening in practice. In this context we can note that the Integrated Children's System was developed in response to the findings from research, inspections and inquiry reports that highlighted weaknesses in practice in a number of key areas, including recording (Social Services Inspectorate 1999; Walker *et al.* 2003a), assessment (Cleaver *et al.* 2004b; Social Services Inspectorate 1999), planning (Cleaver *et al.* 2004b) and review (Grimshaw and Sinclair 1997). The recent report into the death of Victoria Climbié stressed the failure of practitioners and managers to carry out basic practice tasks.

On this basis the level of change required by authorities to implement the Integrated Children's System could be considered to be significant, particularly so given the aims of the scheme to (a) impact decisively on outcomes-led interventions of greater organisational visibility, (b) offer management more accessible and better information to assist supervision and resource allocation and (c) enhance opportunities for strategic thinking and inter-agency working.

To repeat, although the implementation of the Integrated Children's System did not introduce any new legislative or policy requirements, it did involve a marked change in the way that practitioners and managers across children's social care recorded, organised and used information in relation to individuals and groups of children; that is, a change to the core business of the organisation. The organisational structure and culture of children's social care and the scale and type of change indicated that implementation would present the pilot authorities with a major challenge which would have to be carefully managed if implementation was to be successful.

Managing implementation

Because the Integrated Children's System was a new initiative few staff, regardless of their position in the organisation, had a comprehensive under-standing of how it would impact on their organisation and the work of their staff. Moreover, trainers, whether local authority based or independent, would not have the experience necessary to train managers and practitioners in using it. The research design recognised the challenge that implementation would present to the pilot authorities and incorporated time to introduce local authorities to the Integrated Children's System and to carry out much of the training delivered to local authority managers and practitioners, during the early stages of implementation (see Appendix 1 for details on training).

Before identifying the actions taken by the local authorities at each stage in implementing the Integrated Children's System it is important to review how they managed the process of change.

Ensuring senior commitment

Research on the introduction of Looking After Children (Jones *et al.* 1998; Ward 1995a) and the Assessment Framework (Cleaver *et al.* 2004a) high-lighted the importance of senior level commitment to successful implementa-tion. This finding informed the process used to select local authorities for the study. To qualify for selection, senior managers from all key agencies working with children in the potential pilot authority had to provide a written commit-ment to piloting the Integrated Children's System.

Strategic inter-agency groups

Once selected, each pilot authority made use of an existing strategic inter-agency group, such as their Children's Services Planning Group or their Children and Young People's Partnership, to keep senior managers informed of developments and progress. However, in no authority did the existing strategic inter-agency group take the lead on implementation. There appear to have been two main reasons to explain this. First, the strategic nature of these groups meant that they were unable to dedicate the time necessary to support implementation. Second, the implementation of the Integrated Children's System impacted most directly and significantly on children's social care. However, to establish it successfully as an inter-agency initiative all of the pilot authorities stressed the importance of locating the Integrated Children's System within a strategic inter-agency framework and keeping these groups informed.

Project groups

In each pilot authority the process of implementation was led by a smaller project group drawn from staff within children's social care. The implementation groups were responsible for:

- identifying the key factors that may impact on implementation at a local level
- audits of equipment and practice
- developing a timetable and plan for implementation
- promoting ownership of the Integrated Children's System
- developing a communications strategy
- drawing up training programmes (intra- and inter-agency) to support implementation
- revising existing policies, procedural guidance and protocols as appropriate
- monitoring the process of implementation
- establishing quality control and assurance systems
- developing information for children and families which explains the Integrated Children's System.

Membership of implementation groups differed between the pilot authorities but all had representatives from practice, business or administrative services, and IT. The pilot authorities emphasised that implementation had to be taken forward through a partnership between all three of these areas.

Lead officers

All of the authorities identified a lead officer responsible for implementing the Integrated Children's System. In the three English pilot authorities the lead officer came from a practice background while in the Welsh authority the lead officer had a business/administrative background.

Two authorities (the Shire County and the London Borough) released the lead officer of all other duties. While this policy increased the management time available to implement the Integrated Children's System, it also resulted in experienced managers being removed from the core business of children's social care. The other two authorities pursued a different route; the lead officer continued to manage part or all of his or her existing responsibilities. However, the scale of the task and the degree of change needed to implement the Integrated Children's System made this difficult and there was a greater reliance on other members of the implementation group to take forward key tasks in these authorities. All of the lead officers had regular contact with the senior manager for children's social care and members of the senior management team.

The process of implementation

The model for managing change in public services developed by Docherty and Horne (2002) provides a useful framework for analysing the processes of implementation across the four pilot authorities. The model is based on a project management approach to change, a method used in all four authorities. Such an approach is suited to 'the achievement of a carefully defined series of objectives in a logical sequence over a period of time' (Docherty and Horne 2002, p.78). The model has five stages:

- Defining: This phase involves translating the broad objectives of the initiative into clearly defined and measurable objectives.
- Resourcing: This phase identifies the level of resources, financial, equipment and personnel, that will be required to implement the change.
- Planning: During this phase the objectives of implementation are broken down into tasks. Each task is prioritised, given a timescale and allocated to a group or individual. Tasks that have to happen

in sequence are identified, along with those that may take place in parallel.

- Implementation: This phase involves the management of the implementation processes, keeping track of each task, and anticipating and responding to issues that may arise.

- Evaluation: The final phase reflects on the previous four stages to identify what went well and identifies areas where consolidation may be required and lessons for the future.

Defining

The Integrated Children's System was an initiative led by central government; consequently local authorities were not responsible for defining it. The Integrated Children's System was defined by its three components:

- a conceptual framework for assessment, planning, intervention and review

- a set of data requirements for children's services in relation to children in need and their families

- exemplars of case records. (See Chapter 1 for more details.)

The set of data requirements was developed to support local authorities in planning their IT systems. The goal for the pilot authorities was to implement the Integrated Children's System in an electronic format across children's social care within the six- to seven-month timescale required by the research.

Resources

The pilot authorities were not provided with any additional funding to support them to introduce the Integrated Children's System and the costs associated with implementation had to be met from existing resources. A capital grant, paid over three years, was provided by the government to support all local authorities implement the Integrated Children's System during 2004/5.

No detailed information was gathered in relation to costs but the pilot authorities reported that the main expenses were in relation to: the development of and purchase of IT systems; releasing staff for training; supporting the process of implementation (in two authorities this included the funding of specific project lead officers); and purchasing equipment.

In order to identify the scale of the task and the resources required, all the authorities undertook a series of audits. These included audits of:

- existing practice and business processes
- IT provision and staff skills
- social work practice.

EXISTING PRACTICE AND BUSINESS PROCESSES

Pilot authorities reported that understanding existing practice and business processes was essential to ensure that these were incorporated into the IT systems developed to support the Integrated Children's System. Authorities found that 'process mapping' (process mapping covers issues such as: what work is done and by whom, what gets recorded and by whom, and when the recording is made) enabled them to rationalise current processes. As a result one authority (the London Borough) reported that they had been able to reduce the number of records that could be completed by practitioners from just over 100 to 40.

All four pilot authorities found that process mapping took much longer than anticipated. The delays arose for two reasons. First, local authorities had mistakenly assumed that major revisions would not be required to bring existing processes into line with the Integrated Children's System. Second, the time taken to develop an effective IT system was underestimated; IT systems do not accommodate ambiguity and all possible processes had to be anticipated and built into the system.

IT PROVISION AND STAFF SKILLS

Authorities had to implement the Integrated Children's System in an electronic format and therefore IT was central to successful implementation. Each of the pilot authorities undertook three audits in relation to IT provision and staff skills:

1. Current IT systems were reviewed to:
   - assess the extent to which existing systems were compatible with the data and other requirements of the Integrated Children's System
   - identify whether existing systems could be developed to incorporate the requirements of the Integrated Children's

System or whether a new system would have to be commissioned

- o identify the financial and technical resources to undertake the necessary changes

- o identify how relevant data could be migrated from the existing IT system to the revised/new IT system.

2. Existing IT provision was reviewed to establish whether:

- o all teams and establishments were linked to the organisation's IT system and could access or input data as required

- o there were sufficient computers in each team and establishment to allow easy access for workers inputting data

- o existing computers had the technical capacity to operate the new or revised IT system.

3. The IT skills of staff across the service were audited to:

- o assess the skills levels within each team and establishment

- o identify which team members had key skills and could be used as 'champions' to advise and support other team members

- o determine which team members had few skills and plan any additional support they may require.

The introduction of the Integrated Children's System coincided with major developments in both IT system user interface and the application of form technology. While holding out the promise of much wider and simpler accessibility, web- or intranet-based technologies represent a significant jump both for local authorities and for software developers. Consequently both local authorities and software suppliers tended to wait for details of the new system before making substantial new investment. Even when details of the Integrated Children's System and draft exemplars were published, authorities tended to hold back while awaiting the 'definitive version', for fear of incurring additional IT costs.

At the start of the research all four pilot authorities had IT systems for children's services in place which needed to be tailored to support the Integrated Children's System. In three authorities (the Shire County, the Welsh Local Authority and the Unitary Authority) these were in-house IT systems. Following an audit of their systems all three concluded that they could be developed to meet the requirements of the Integrated Children's System. However, the Unitary Authority experienced problems with their upgraded

in-house IT system that resulted in them entering into a development partnership with a commercial IT supplier. They believed this partnership would be
more cost effective and result in a better quality system which would be more
sustainable over time. However, the changeover interrupted the implementation timetable and initially undermined staff confidence. The two remaining
authorities took different approaches in developing and tailoring their
in-house IT systems. The Shire County commissioned an IT consultant to
work with them in developing their IT solution to support the Integrated
Children's System, as internal capacity was limited. In contrast the Welsh
Local Authority carried out all their development work in-house.

Unlike the other three pilot authorities the IT system used by the
London Borough had been developed by a commercial supplier. Implementation of the Integrated Children's System in this authority was not
determined by the timetable for the research, but by their need to replace
their existing IT system, a system that would end its technical life by
March 2003 just before the start of the pilot period. Enquiries revealed
that the system provider was only willing to sell the authority a three-year
extension. This option was not considered to be economic by the authority. In response authority entered into a development partnership with
another systems provider to develop their IT solution for the Integrated
Children's System. This gave the authority an absolute deadline of April
2003 to implement the new system; after that date they would have no
operational IT system. The authority reported that they had begun preparation for implementation prior to being selected as a pilot site.

The two authorities, the Unitary Authority and the London Borough,
which had purchased their IT system from commercial suppliers, formed a
'development partnership' with the supplier. This partnership secured the
pilot authority preferential treatment and the possibility of greater support
and customisation, while the supplier obtained a test-bed for a new or substantially upgraded product to support the Integrated Children's System. The
partnerships, however, were not free of problems. The pilot authorities found
that their needs were sometimes placed behind those of a wider customer base
for whom Integrated Children's System functionality was not yet a priority;
frequent and sometimes unstable software upgrades consumed scarce IT
resources and sapped the morale of users; new features were sometimes poorly
documented; the user interface might not be geared to local requirements; and
customisation facilities (for instance management consoles) were sometimes
missing. On the other hand using a system purchased from a commercial

supplier may benefit the authorities in the longer term as they will profit from the continuing development of the IT system and further releases of software.

SOCIAL WORK PRACTICE

To identify the impact of implementing the Integrated Children's System on practice, pilot authorities also undertook limited audits of social work case files. The file audits were used to identify practice processes, the extent to which national and local regulations and guidance were being followed, and gaps in practice skills (for example in relation to recording and assessment). Authorities also identified possible skills gaps by reviewing the provision and take up of training provided in relation to practice.

Planning

Authorities emphasised that to be successful implementation plans must be based on a clear understanding of what is happening, rather than an assumption of what should be happening.

All of the authorities reported that the timescale required by the research had not allowed them sufficient time to plan effectively and prepare for the implementation of the Integrated Children's System. Authorities commented that they would have welcomed additional time for process mapping, to audit practice, and to undertake training in relation to practice.

Each authority stressed the importance of adopting a structured project management approach to implementation. In addition to a lead officer and implementation group this approach had two other key elements:

- a clear written project plan with timescales which placed key tasks in the process of implementation in sequence to allow progress to be monitored
- an issues log that identified factors that may impact on implementation.

The pilot authorities used a range of strategies to inform and involve staff throughout the agency. These included focus groups, briefing papers, visits to teams by the lead officer and members of the implementation group, champions or super-users and users groups for specific areas of practice, such as looked after children.

Implementation

The pilot authorities had been selected because of their strengths in terms of practice, inter-agency working and use of IT (see Appendix 1 for more details on selection). It was anticipated that this would ensure that they would be able to implement the Integrated Children's System within the relatively brief timeframe of six to seven months.

TIMESCALES

The implementation of the Integrated Children's System proved to be a more complex task and involved a greater degree of change than had been anticipated; only the London Borough implemented within the agreed timescale. As already discussed the driver for implementation within this authority was the requirement to replace their existing IT system. The three other pilot authorities all experienced considerable delays. The Welsh Local Authority was able to implement within six months of the agreed research timescale, and the Shire County initiated a roll-out programme which was completed two months later. In contrast the Unitary Authority experienced greater difficulties. Initially it was thought implementation had been successfully completed eight months after the agreed timescale. However, severe technical difficulties with their IT system meant that despite the efforts of staff within the authority they were unable to implement before the end of the research project.

These delays in implementation resulted principally from the complexity of the IT systems and related to both developmental and technical issues. Developmental issues included the time required for detailed process mapping of local practice as mentioned earlier. Technical issues related to the inconsistencies between exemplars, in both language and format, which had to be resolved before they could be built into the system. The timescale of the pilot allowed only limited time to build and test IT systems and as a result authorities encountered a range of technical issues. All of the authorities that implemented the Integrated Children's System reported that there was insufficient time for system testing and consequently, when systems were implemented, practitioners continued to encounter technical problems.

TRAINING

The pilot authorities reported that training needed to be a continuous process and should not end with the introduction of the Integrated Children's

System. Authorities identified that to be effective training should cover three areas:

- the background to and principles underpinning the Integrated Children's System
- changes in practice
- newly introduced IT systems.

Authorities stressed the importance of training staff on the principles underpinning the development of the system. Training in this area helped staff to see the Integrated Children's System (a) as primarily a practice initiative underpinned by an IT system and (b) to recognise that it is a continuing development of previous initiatives. The value of this training was highlighted by the experience of the London Borough whose agenda for implementation was driven by their need to quickly replace their existing IT system. The timetable for the new IT system did not allow the authority time to train staff on the principles underpinning the Integrated Children's System prior to its introduction. Consequently, many staff within the authority viewed the Integrated Children's System as an IT development and, when issues arose, were unable to distinguish between those which had their basis in practice and those related to IT. For example, the research team were told that the Referral and Information Record was not suited to the needs of practitioners. However, subsequent discussion revealed that the issue was not related to the content of the record but the length of time it initially took to load on the authority's IT system.

Authorities reported that the timescale for implementation meant that it was difficult to undertake all the necessary training in relation to practice, although some of the pilots used delays in implementation to extend their training programme.

All authorities provided training for staff on their new IT systems. This was planned to ensure that any delay between staff receiving the training and using the new system was minimised. However, the scale of the project and its technical aspects meant that achieving co-ordination could be difficult. For example, in the Unitary Authority training had to be rescheduled six times because of changes in the authority's date for implementation.

Pilot authorities reported that they had introduced a number of ways to support staff to use IT including:

- training programmes

- on-site support through members of the Integrated Children's System project group, specialist IT staff or champions
- IT help-lines
- IT practice manuals.

Administrative staff played an important role in supporting practitioners, particularly those with limited IT skills, to use the system. Administrative staff were also key to quality control, through checking whether records had been completed and the accuracy of key data.

The scale of the training presented the pilot authorities with an enormous challenge. In response, authorities used a cascade approach, training 'champions' who were responsible for training other members of their team. Champions were drawn mainly from volunteer practitioners and administrative staff. Although champions could offer considerable support to practitioners, securing the necessary numbers proved difficult. For example, authorities were not always able to easily recruit staff to take on the role of champion and, once recruited, authorities found it difficult to release them from their existing duties. Consequently, in most authorities the work undertaken by champions was in addition to their normal duties and their availability to provide immediate hands-on support, which was valued by practitioners, was limited. A more comprehensive training programme was required. However, providing the necessary level of training placed a considerable strain on the resources of the training section and on the capacity of teams to carry out their core business when staff were released for training.

Authorities reported that they had also revised their induction training for new staff to ensure it included the Integrated Children's System and the IT system that supported it.

COMMUNICATION

A range of strategies were used in the authorities to inform and involve staff throughout the agency. These included focus groups, briefing papers, visits to teams by the lead officer and members of the implementation group and establishing users groups for specific areas of practice, for example looked after children. Champions or super-users also played an important role in disseminating information about the Integrated Children's System and implementation plans. Their role was more effective when they were identified and involved at an early stage.

INTER-AGENCY WORKING

Pilot authorities reported that they found it difficult to involve other agencies in the Integrated Children's System. Despite inter-agency briefing sessions focusing on how the Integrated Children's System would affect them, partner agencies at the time of the research tended to think that it only had implications for children's social care. The scale of the task meant that authorities often did not have sufficient resources to work closely with other agencies. The involvement of other agencies was supported through:

- establishing an inter-agency steering group
- inter-agency training and briefing sessions
- using specialist staff such as looked after children's health professionals, to act as champions for their agency.

The Welsh Local Authority established a number of agency-specific sub-groups (health, education, police) that explored the potential of sharing information electronically; for example, giving professionals from other agencies the opportunity to access basic information on children they were working with. The information needs of each agency were considered in the sub-group and the potential of the Integrated Children's System to provide this information identified. This approach was very successful in engaging partner agencies. However, the authority reported that it was very resource intensive and in the initial phases it was a case of children's social services giving information and building trust. They reported that as time went on there was increased interest from partner agencies in contributing information.

PROCESS AND APPROACH

The Integrated Children's System was developed to support and facilitate the direct entry of information by practitioners and this was the approach adopted in the three English authorities. The Welsh Local Authority decided that data would initially be entered into the system by administrative staff with social workers taking over once the system was glitch free. This decision was based on current practice and facilitated by higher levels of administrative staff within the teams.

The approach taken to implementation was influenced by the size and circumstances of the local authority. For example, the need to introduce a new IT system quickly meant that in the London Borough the Integrated Children's System was implemented across all of children's social care at the same time.

The Welsh Local Authority implemented on a team-by-team basis (intake, and assessment team, looked after team etc.) within a brief timescale. The Shire County employed a rolling programme of implementation over a two month period area by area. All teams within the area received their training at the same time and the area went live on the same date.

Evaluation

In evaluating their implementation of the Integrated Children's System local authorities commented on the following issues:

- the focus of the implementation strategy
- shortcomings in practice
- mechanisms for quality control and assurance
- resources
- relationships with IT developers
- the exemplars
- enhancements to the System.

THE FOCUS OF THE IMPLEMENTATION STRATEGY

All the pilot authorities reported that the implementation of the Integrated Children's System impacted on every area of social work practice. Authorities recommended that implementation plans should involve all staff including residential, family centre and specialist teams, even where a phased implementation meant that these teams would not be affected until much later. This approach ensured that all staff felt involved in the process of implementation and understood the relevance of the Integrated Children's System to their practice.

All three English authorities reported that during the initial period of implementation the focus was making sure practitioners got to grips with new IT systems and different ways of recording, rather than on ensuring their practice was in line with the principles of the Integrated Children's System. As noted earlier, in the Welsh Local Authority administrative staff were responsible for using the new IT system. There were three main reasons why the English authorities initially focused on IT.

First, staff did not have the required level of IT skills and initial training addressed these shortcomings. The Integrated Children's System requires practitioners to change the way they use computers from simply accessing and entering information into an electronic database (for example, basic information about children such as their name and address) to completing electronic records (such as writing contextual information about the children and analysing this information on screen). This presented many staff with a considerable challenge.

The second reason related to the time restraints. The parameters of the research meant that participating local authorities needed to implement the Integrated Children's System within a six to seven month timetable – getting the IT right took first place.

The third reason was that IT systems were prone to difficulties. The timetable meant that there was insufficient time for the rigorous testing of IT solutions and none were glitch free when released to practitioners. In the Unitary Authority the problems resulted in the system having to be withdrawn. The approach taken in the Welsh Local Authority meant that the administrative staff acted as a ring-fence protecting social work practitioners from the inevitable bugs that arise in any new, complex IT system. Furthermore, administrative staff were better placed to understand IT issues and work with their in-house IT development team to resolve them.

SHORTCOMINGS IN PRACTICE

All the pilot authorities stressed that the Integrated Children's System must not be seen as a solution to existing practice issues; its introduction highlights areas of strong practice and the nature and extent of practice weaknesses. Three main areas of weakness were reported: recording; analysing the information gathered during an assessment; and developing plans with specific outcomes. Authorities sought to address these issues through specific training courses and additional support. However, the need for authorities to comply with the research timetable meant that most of this training was provided after the introduction of the Integrated Children's System. This meant that practice difficulties hampered practitioners' use of the system. The support provided by team managers was, therefore, essential to help practitioners develop these skills and make best use of the Integrated Children's System.

MECHANISMS FOR QUALITY CONTROL AND ASSURANCE

The authorities emphasised the importance of effective quality control and quality assurance mechanisms, particularly at the front end of the system when data is first entered. Front-line managers played a key role, through supervision, in ensuring the quality of the information as well as its accuracy was reviewed. Administrative staff were also used to monitor the quality of data entered into the system. The London Borough and the Shire County reported a gradual shift in the role of administrative staff from supporting practitioners in entering information about children and families to quality assuring what was recorded.

RESOURCES

The authorities reported that considerable resources had to be identified, both financial and staffing, to support implementation. Local authorities found that the need for these resources did not end with the introduction of the Integrated Children's System but continued at the same level after implementation.

RELATIONSHIPS WITH IT DEVELOPERS

Local authorities that used a software house which was supplying an IT solution to support the Integrated Children's System to a number of different local authorities were often frustrated as their requests for assistance or changes were not always prioritised. For example, delays occurred because software was still under development to meet the needs of other authorities. In addition the demands of other customers could influence key features of the system. A suggested solution to some of these difficulties was for authorities using the same IT provider to join forces and agree the key elements of the system specification, thus reducing individual development costs, and increasing their capacity to influence its development.

Pilot authorities working with external providers emphasised the importance of:

- drawing up clear and specific contracts based on legal advice
- entering into early negotiations with IT providers
- ensuring that the IT system includes internal business processes and records and not just the Integrated Children's System exemplars
- having the ability to modify or add records; this will ensure that the system is responsive to local needs, gives the authority greater control of the system, and reduces potential expenditure on changes
- being able to create management reports from the system rather than being obliged to go through the provider.

The authorities that had developed an in-house IT solution to the Integrated Children's System reported greater satisfaction with the development process. They experienced better access to IT developers, which made it easier to create a partnership between IT, business and practice. The in-house developers were able to respond more quickly than commercial suppliers when issues arose, and problems were resolved in a shorter timescale. However, building on an existing in-house IT system was not a low cost option (the Shire County considered that they would need to spend a further £200,000, spread over the next two years, before their system would be fully functional). Additional resources had to be brought in to develop the system and tensions and delays could occur because of the pressure of other demands on the IT department.

THE EXEMPLARS

Within their IT solutions authorities took different approaches to the exemplars. Some used the exemplars as templates for practitioners to input information, that is to say the screen on the computer followed the layout of the exemplars. Others used the exemplars as outputs from the system, that is the screen used to input information did not look like the exemplar but when printed the output record resembled it.

ENHANCEMENTS TO THE SYSTEM

Authorities developed a number of different enhancements to their IT systems to support practitioners. These included:

- practitioner information or management screens, which provided the practitioners with an overview of their caseload and activities
- a case note facility
- workflow elements; these guided practitioners through a particular practice process and ensured that key tasks were completed
- alerts and notifications for practitioners and managers to inform them when tasks were due or overdue
- 'cloning' or copying facilities, which enabled relevant information on one child's record to be copied to the record of another child in the family; the system identified the records that contained 'cloned' elements
- print selection, which allowed practitioners to select the sections of a record that would be printed out.

Summary points

The level of change required by authorities to implement the Integrated Children's System was significant. It involved a marked change in the way practitioners and managers in children's social care record, organise and use information about the children and families with whom they work.

Pilot authorities used existing strategic inter-agency groups to keep other agencies informed of progress. However, because initially the focus was on implementing the system within children's social care, it proved difficult to involve partner agencies fully.

All the pilot authorities adopted a project management approach to implementation. This involved an implementation group, an identified lead officer (although in only two of the authorities was this a dedicated post), a written project plan and an issues log.

Although the membership of the implementation groups varied between the pilot authorities, all included representatives of practice, business/administration and IT.

The role of champions was key to successful implementation and sustained change. It was important to identify champions at an early stage and to ensure they had sufficient time and resources to support colleagues.

To identify the scale of the changes necessary the pilot authorities audited their existing practice and business processes, their IT provision and staff skills, and the social work practice. The findings from the audits enabled local practice processes to be streamlined, and highlighted areas of strong practice and the nature and extent of practice weaknesses.

Prior to implementation all four pilot authorities had an existing electronic information system. In order to implement the Integrated Children's System two authorities developed their existing in-house system. The remaining two authorities entered into development partnerships with different IT providers. Authorities which developed in-house IT solutions expressed a greater degree of satisfaction with their system and reported that technical issues were resolved more quickly.

In preparing staff to use the Integrated Children's System the pilot authorities stressed that training must cover: background and principles underpinning the Integrated Children's System; changes in practice; and the new IT system.

To support staff to use unfamiliar IT systems authorities introduced training programmes, on-site support, IT helplines and IT practice manuals. Induction training was also revised to cover the Integrated Children's System.

The Integrated Children's System requires practitioners to change the way they use computers from simply accessing and entering information to completing electronic records. The front-line managers played a key role in ensuring the quality and accuracy of the recorded information.

Implementing the Integrated Children's System incurred costs in relation to the development of and purchase of IT systems, releasing staff for training and supporting the process of implementation. Authorities who developed their own IT systems reported that this was not always a cheaper option.

Only one pilot authority implemented the Integrated Children's System within the agreed six month timescale. Two implemented with a six month delay and one had not fully implemented by the end of the research study. Delays in implementation were primarily the result of technical issues relating to the IT systems. Pilot authorities working with external providers emphasised the importance of developing clear and specific contracts based on legal advice.

During the pilot the authorities developed a range of enhancements to their IT systems to support staff, including management screens, case note facilities, alerts and print selection.

Chapter 3

Impact of the Integrated Children's System on Recording Social Work Practice

Introduction

A key factor that informed the development of the Integrated Children's System was the need to improve social work recording for children in need, an issue highlighted in inspections (Social Services Inspectorate 1998). To be able to measure a child's progress or the impact of services over time depends on routinely gathering and recording information on the child's development within the context of their family and the community in which they live. Information about children in need (as defined by the Children Act 1989) should be collected and reviewed in the same way regardless of the services provided or the organisation or agency responsible for providing the service. To address this the Integrated Children's System introduces a set of exemplar records designed to reflect the core processes of information gathering, assessment, planning and reviewing within children's social care (Department of Health and Department for Education and Skills 2000–2005, Briefing Paper 5).

This chapter explores the impact of the Integrated Children's System on recorded social work practice. To do this, information was gathered from social work case files prior to its introduction to establish a baseline (audit 1) and then again at a period of at least six months after implementation (audit 2). In the first audit, the information was gathered from all records on children's social care case files. For the second audit, the main source was the information contained within each authority's Integrated Children's System. This strategy provided insights into how the authorities had implemented the Integrated Children's System and at what points in the delivery of services to children and families implementation resulted in the greatest challenge or change. A full discussion of the methods can be found in Appendix 1.

Selection and characteristics of cases

Assessing the impact of the Integrated Children's System on social work practice depended on authorities implementing their system six months prior to the second study audit. Unfortunately, in the Unitary Authority implementation was delayed beyond the agreed timescale due to technical difficulties with their IT system (see Chapter 2 for details). The following analysis is, therefore, based on data collected from the London Borough, the Shire County and the Welsh Local Authority.

A structured sample of approximately 50 cases from each participating authority made up the study cohort. The criteria for inclusion were that more than one agency or organisation was involved and that children and families were receiving different types of intervention for different purposes.

The objective was to include a similar number of cases from each of the following groups:

- children with complex needs living at home
- children on the Child Protection Register
- children looked after
- young people looked after who have a Pathway Plan
- disabled children and young people.

To select the cases each authority provided a list of all cases open on an identified date that fell into each particular group. The research team used this sample to identify systematically cases that fitted the study criteria (see Appendix 1 for more information).

A total of 150 cases (577 records) were scrutinised at audit 1 and 143 (785 records) at audit 2. Cases were fairly equally split between the five case groups, as Table 3.1 shows.

Table 3.1 Breakdown of cases included in the two case file samples

	Audit 1	Audit 2
Cases of children with complex needs living at home	29	33
Cases where the child's name is on the Child Protection Register	27	29
Cases where the child is looked after	36	38
Cases of looked after young people with a Pathway Plan	26	20
Cases involving a disabled child	32	23
TOTAL	150 cases (577 exemplars)	143 cases (785 exemplars)

The characteristics of the two samples were relatively similar in terms of gender and age, as Table 3.2 demonstrates. Information about the child's ethnicity had been recorded in 82 per cent of cases in the first audit and in 90 per cent in the second. This data showed that, where information was available, the majority of children and young people in both samples were white British (88% and 84% respectively). The remaining children came from a range of different backgrounds including Asian, Caribbean, African, European and mixed heritage.

General picture of implementation

Before discussing the findings it is important to re-cap briefly on the implementation strategies (described in Chapter 2) adopted by the three participating authorities because they provide a context to the findings.

Development of the system in the Welsh Local Authority was in-house and implementation was led by administrative staff who initially entered the data onto the system; the plan was for social workers to take on this role at a later stage. As has been discussed, the benefits of this approach were that early teething problems were experienced by a small group of staff rather than the wider workforce and social workers could continue to focus on practice issues. However, there was concern that the process of implementation lost sight of the child or young person. Generally, introduction of the Integrated

Table 3.2 Characteristics of the two case file samples

Gender		
	Audit 1 (n=150)	Audit 2 (n=143)
Male	52%	51%
Female	47%	49%
Unborn	1%	—
Age		
Unborn	3%	1%
0–2 years	11%	17%
3–4 years	11%	4%
5–9 years	16%	17%
10–14 years	27%	29%
15 and older	32%	32%

Children's System in this authority led to an improvement in the amount of information recorded, with many sections of the records completed more frequently. Furthermore, in this authority there were real improvements in the quality of the information recorded.

The London Borough implemented the Integrated Children's System earlier than the other authorities due to the external pressures encountered through changing software suppliers. The time constraints resulted in a focus on IT at the expense of practice issues; winning the 'hearts and minds' of practitioners took second place. The impact of the Integrated Children's System in the London Borough appears mixed: some documentation was completed more fully, for other documents the quantity and quality of recording remained unchanged, and some were completed less comprehensively.

In the Shire County an external software consultant was commissioned to develop their IT system. This was the last of the three authorities to implement and only completed implementation three to four months before the second audit was undertaken. Although the second audit was delayed from its original timetable to take account of this authority's later implementation, it meant that data gathered post implementation was during a period when staff were still familiarising themselves with new practice processes and IT systems. In this authority, a number of records showed a decrease in the rate and quality of recording.

Feedback from managers in the participating authorities suggests that deterioration reflects the process of having to learn new systems and is, by definition, temporary. For example, managers spoke of the need to break through a 'barrier' with regard to implementation. Once through, the focus for practitioners and managers shifts from the implementation of IT and new processes back to practice issues. Implementation of the Integrated Children's System has made both good and bad practice transparent; as one project manager said, 'you can run, but you can't hide.'

Findings: Children with complex needs

The Integrated Children's System builds on the Framework for the Assessment of Children in Need and their Families (Department of Health *et al.* 2000a). This provided guidance primarily for professionals and other staff involved in undertaking assessments of children in need under the Children Act 1989 and included a set of records for gathering and analysing information (Department of Health and Cleaver 2000). As such, work with children in need has not undergone major changes with the implementation of the Integrated Children's System.

Information gathering

The Integrated Children's System introduced very few changes to the Referral and Initial Information Record (introduced with the Assessment Framework) and has three functions:

- to record the source and reason for a referral or request for services
- to record the response of social services and other relevant agencies to the referral or request for services
- to provide a record of essential information about a child or young person.

(Department of Health and Department for Education and Skills 2000–2005, Briefing Paper No.5, pp.2–3)

Research suggests that prior to the implementation of the Integrated Children's System key information, such as the reason for and source of the referral, and the identity of the child and his or her carers, was recorded in most cases (Cleaver *et al.* 2004b). However, parental awareness of the referral was less likely to be recorded.

The present study is based on a scrutiny of 175 referrals, 84 recorded prior to the implementation of the Integrated Children's System and 91 recorded post implementation. In both audits there was a variety of reasons that had resulted in the child and family being referred to children's services and those cited most often were child protection concerns, parental alcohol and drug misuse, domestic abuse and disabilities. The findings show that overall the information recorded on the Referral and Information Record did not change substantially with the introduction of the Integrated Children's System. However, there were significant improvements in two areas.

One area of improvement was recording whether parents were aware of a referral. Prior to the implementation of the Integrated Children's System this information had been recorded in 58 per cent of cases (a rate similar to that identified by Cleaver *et al.* 2004b); post implementation this figure had risen to 85 per cent. Recording whether parents or carers are aware of the referral is an indication of the priority practitioners give to working in partnership with parents because this information will influence how the family is approached.

The other area of improvement was recording the outcome of a referral. Prior to local authorities implementing the Integrated Children's System the outcome of the referral was noted in 48 per cent of cases; after implementation this was recorded in practically every case (96%). Recording the outcome of a referral is essential to understand both the result of the referral and the take-up of services.

Assessment

The main change introduced to assessing children in need is the greater emphasis on planning both at the initial and core assessment stage.

THE INITIAL ASSESSMENT

> The Initial Assessment Record is the record of an initial assessment, the decisions and actions resulting from the assessment including an Initial Plan for the Child. (Department of Health and Department for Education and Skills 2000–2005, Briefing Paper No.5, p.4)

The Integrated Children's System introduces a linked Initial Plan for the Child following an initial assessment. This innovation enables the impact of services on children's development and welfare to be reviewed. The Initial Plan was introduced in response to feedback from practitioners following implementation of the Assessment Framework.

The sample included 133 Initial Assessment Records, 50 recorded prior to the implementation of the Integrated Children's System and 83 completed post implementation.

The scrutiny of the records suggests a trend towards less information being recorded on the initial assessment, although this was not found to be statistically significant. For example, information on a child's developmental needs fell from being recorded on 80 per cent of records at audit 1 to 70 per cent of records at audit 2, parenting capacity from 83 per cent to 70 per cent, and the family and environmental factors from 86 per cent to 69 per cent. However, separating out the authorities shows that the decline in recording in the Shire County skewed the findings; the rate of recording for the other two authorities showed little change. As explained earlier this authority implemented the Integrated Children's System later than the others and as a result practitioners had less experience of their system. At the time audit 2 was being carried out social work practitioners were still grappling with new IT and recording methods.

Prior to the Integrated Children's System the initial assessment was not linked to a formal plan. Social work practitioners recorded the outcome of the initial assessment (for example, core assessment or strategy discussion) but not the actions and services that were to be provided to the child and family. In consequence, data about the Initial Plan could only be gathered following the implementation of the Integrated Children's System.

With the introduction of the Integrated Children's System, an Initial Plan is completed when the practitioner decides that further action or services need to be provided or co-ordinated by children's social care. The findings suggest that 45 per cent of cases progressed in this way. Where an Initial Plan was recorded in the majority of cases (81.6%) the plan was rated as 'specific' by the research team. To be rated as 'specific' the plan had to clearly identify the child's needs, relate these to specific objectives with tasks allocated and a timetable outlined.

CORE ASSESSMENTS

A core assessment provides a structured, in-depth assessment of the child's needs where his or her circumstances are complex. A completed Core Assessment Record is then used to develop the Child's Plan. When a child becomes looked after, an up to date core assessment is required and is used to inform the child's first Care Plan. (*ibid.*, Briefing Paper No.5, p.4)

A total of 103 Core Assessment Records were included in the study: 47 had been completed prior to the implementation of the Integrated Children's System and 56 post implementation.

Amalgamating the data from all three local authorities would suggest that the introduction of the Integrated Children's System has resulted in a decrease in the amount of information recorded on the Core Assessment Record. However, separating out the findings in the three authorities reveals once again that recording practice in the Shire County (the authority which had most recently implemented the Integrated Children's System) skewed the figures. The following examples contrast the recording practice of this authority and the other two, for both specific information and more complex issues.

- The cases with information on immunisations reduced from 100 per cent to 56 per cent whereas the rates of completion stayed the same for the remaining two authorities at 80 per cent and 65 per cent.

- The cases where information was recorded on whether a 'young person has been/is pregnant or has fathered a child' fell from 100 per cent to 78 per cent whereas the rates of completion reduced slightly in the second authority from 92 per cent to 82 per cent and stayed the same for the third at 90 per cent.

- The cases with information on the child's developmental needs, parenting capacity and family and environmental factors fell from 100 per cent to 48 per cent whereas the rates of completion stayed similar in the other two authorities at 94 per cent.

Although the rate of recording information on many areas of the core assessment decreased in the Shire County with the implementation of the Integrated Children's System (in contrast to the other pilot authorities), the quality of recording remained high for all three, a finding that should be applauded (approximately 80 per cent of the recording was rated by the research team as having been well done both before and after implementation). For a dimension to be rated as 'well done' the social worker had to record some information against at least three-quarters of the issues noted on the Core Assessment Record.

Child's Plan

The key change to the core assessment was the separation of the Child's Plan from the assessment record. The plan had previously been an integral part of the core assessment when the Assessment Framework was first introduced in 2000, but the two were separated in response to subsequent feedback from local authorities.

> A Child's Plan is completed following a core assessment. The format for a Child's Plan is more detailed and will revise and replace the Initial Plan for a child.

> A Child's Plan is the Child Protection Plan for a child whose name has been placed on the local child protection register. A Child's Plan will still be required for a child who has had his or her name removed from a Child Protection Register, or who has ceased to be looked after but remains a child in need who is in receipt of social services. (*ibid.*, Briefing Paper No.5, p.6)

A total of 65 Child's Plans were included in the study, 30 completed prior to the implementation and 35 post implementation.

The implementation of the Integrated Children's System resulted in more detailed information being recorded on the Child's Plan. For example, increases in the amount of information were noted both in relation to the overall aim of the plan (30 per cent in audit 1 compared with 71 per cent in audit 2 – significant at $p<0.001$) and type of plan; that is, whether an 'in need plan' or 'child protection plan' (77 per cent compared with 97 per cent).

Increases were also found in the amount of information recorded on the child's developmental needs, parenting capacity, and wider family and environmental factors. The quality of recording children's developmental needs remained high. However, it is of some concern that the quality of recording parenting capacity and family and environmental factors declined. For example, pre implementation in 77 per cent of cases the quality of information on parenting capacity was classified by the research team as 'well done' but only 55 per cent met this criteria post implementation. Similarly, although 63 per cent of recording on wider family and environmental factors was rated as 'well done' pre the Integrated Children's System this rate fell to 44 per cent post Integrated Children's System (see Table 3.3).

Table 3.3 Information recorded on Child's Plans

	Audit 1 (n=30)	Audit 2 (n=35)
Child's development needs		
Health	60%, of which 95% completed well	97%,[1] of which 88% completed well
Education	67%, of which 85% completed well	71%, of which 80% completed well
Emotional and behavioural development	60%, of which 83% completed well	69%, of which 83% completed well
Identity	50%, of which 80% completed well	57%, of which 80% completed well
Family and social relationships	53%, of which 88% completed well	54%, of which 74% completed well
Social presentation	43%, of which 85% completed well	51%, of which 78% completed well
Self-care skills	47%, of which 86% completed well	46%, of which 75% completed well
Parenting capacity of birth family	73%, of which 77% completed well	89%, of which 55% completed well
Wider family and environmental factors of birth family	63%, of which 63% completed well	77%, of which 44% completed well

Reviewing

To review the outcome of a child in need is not a statutory function of children's social care and, prior to the Integrated Children's System, no formal process to undertake this task existed. To address this, the Integrated Children's System introduced the Child in Need Review. However, during the early stages of the pilot, local authorities concentrated most of their efforts on implementing records relating to their statutory functions, such as child protection and looked after children reviews. Once these were in place authorities were able to turn their attention to introducing the review for children in

---

1   t-tests for equality of means shows difference is significant at $p < 0.001$.

need. As a result, too few Child in Need Review records were found at the time of the research, in order to present any meaningful findings.

Discussion

The Integrated Children's System brought about few alterations to the records for recording referrals and assessments of children in need that had been introduced as part of the Assessment Framework in 2000. As a result it has had little impact on most aspects of recording practice. Where a new record has been introduced such as the Child's Plan, the findings show a trend for more information to be recorded on all three domains of children's lives (developmental needs, parenting capacity, and family and environmental factors). However, there is no room for complacency, for although information about a child's health and education was recorded in over 70 per cent of cases, information on children's family and social relationships, social presentation and self-care skills was still only found in approximately half the cases. This pattern of focusing more on health and education is repeated across other plans developed for children receiving different types and levels of services.

Findings: Children in need of protection

This part of the system was subject to significant change with the introduction of the Integrated Children's System. For some child protection processes, such as strategy discussions, it introduced a clear format for recording and for others it replaced existing records in use within local authorities, shifting the emphasis from gathering information about sibling groups to gathering information about individual children.

Information gathering and assessment

Prior to the implementation of the Integrated Children's System there was no standardisation in the way information was recorded for children in need of protection. Local authorities used a variety of formats which resulted in information being recorded and stored in different places on the case file in different authorities and in some cases within the same authority, creating difficulties in locating key data quickly. For example, only one authority had a standard format for recording strategy discussions across the authority. In the other authorities discussions could be recorded as case notes, meetings or on local formats. The Integrated Children's System introduced specific exemplars to support planning and decision making at the key stages of the child protection process (outlined in Working Together, HM Government 2006c, and What To Do if You're Worried a Child is Being Abused, HM Government 2006e) such as the strategy discussion, section 47 enquiries, initial child protection conference, and child protection conference review.

RECORD OF STRATEGY DISCUSSION

> The Record of Strategy Discussion records the decisions made at a strategy discussion/meeting. (*ibid.*, Briefing Paper No.5, p.5)

The implementation of the Integrated Children's System increased the number of Records of Strategy Discussion (from 4 to 35). Unfortunately, so few records were found on case files before implementation that no comparisons were possible.

However, scrutinising the records completed post implementation shows a high rate of recording. Of 35 Records of Strategy Discussion, 91 per cent recorded the outcome of the discussion. Furthermore, the detail on the recording of further actions was rated as specific by the researchers in 84 per cent of cases. To be rated as specific the record had to have noted the actions, and identified the individuals responsible for further action and timescales.

RECORD OF OUTCOME OF S47 ENQUIRIES

> This records the outcome of s47 enquiries and concurrent core assessment which was instigated following a strategy discussion or meeting. It sets out the further actions to be taken after the s47 enquiries have been completed. (*ibid.*, Briefing Paper No.5, p.6)

The implementation of the Integrated Children's System increased the rate social workers completed a Record of Outcome of s47 Enquiries, rising from 3 to 26. Once again the numbers are too small for any comparisons to be made.

Of the 26 Records of Outcome of s47 Enquiries examined in case files post implementation, the outcome of enquiries was recorded in all but one case (96%). The findings again suggest that the implementation of the Integrated Children's System improved both the rate of recording information and the quality of the information recorded. Recording was rated as specific by the researchers in 88 per cent of cases. Records were classed as specific when the record noted the actions to be taken and the identified responsible person/agency, timescales and the findings.

INITIAL CHILD PROTECTION CONFERENCE REPORT

> This provides a summary of the information gathered by social services prior to an initial child protection conference. This information is used to inform decisions made at the conference and if the child's name is placed on a child protection register, the outline child protection plan. (*ibid.*, Briefing Paper No.5, p.6)

The sample included 79 Initial Child Protection Conference Reports, 36 completed prior to implementation and 43 post implementation. The findings suggest that implementation of the Integrated Children's System has improved recording practice. For example, the quantity of information recorded in the Initial Child Protection Conference Report increased for each of the three domains: the child's developmental needs (63% to 80%, parenting capacity (90% to 95%) and family and environmental factors (78% to 98%).

Previous research indicates that the aspect of assessment that provides the greatest challenge to social work practitioners is the analysis of the information they have gathered (Cleaver *et al.* 2004b). The current findings suggest that the quality of analysis has improved with the implementation of the Integrated Children's System. For example, before the Integrated Children's System only 13 per cent of the Initial Child Protection Conference Reports included an analysis that identified both the needs of the child and recorded the services that were to be provided, compared with 67 per cent[2] post implementation.

CHILD PROTECTION REVIEW

The findings on the impact of the Integrated Children's System on recording the Child Protection Review mirrored those for the Initial Child Protection Conference Report. In general, the Integrated Children's System required practitioners to record detailed information and the result was that more and better quality information was recorded post implementation on children's developmental needs (see Table 3.4).

---

2 t-tests for equality of means shows difference is significant at $p<0.001$.

Table 3.4 Information recorded on Child Protection Reviews

	Audit 1 (n=32)	Audit 2 (n=22)
Child's development needs		
Health	66%, of which 48% completed well	95%, of which 81%[3] completed well
Education	50%, of which 63% completed well	82%, of which 61% completed well
Emotional and behavioural development	56%, of which 33% completed well	82%, of which 67%[4] completed well
Identity	25%, of which 13% completed well	77%,[5] of which 59%[6] completed well
Family and social relationships	56%, of which 39% completed well	82%, of which 56%[7] completed well
Social presentation	44%, of which 14% completed well	82%,[8] of which 67% completed well
Self-care skills	34%, of which 36% completed well	64%, of which 50% completed well
Parenting capacity of birth family	84%, of which 52% completed well	96%, of which 52% completed well
Wider family and environmental factors of birth family	78%, of which 44% completed well	84%, of which 42% completed well

For the researchers to class a section of the record as having been completed well information had to be recorded for each heading on the record for a particular developmental need. For example, in relation to health the following information would have to be recorded:

---

3   t-tests for equality of means shows difference is significant at p<0.001.
4   t-tests for equality of means shows difference is significant at p<0.001.
5   t-tests for equality of means shows difference is significant at p<0.001.
6   t-tests for equality of means shows difference is significant at p<0.001.
7   t-tests for equality of means shows difference is significant at p<0.001.
8   t-tests for equality of means shows difference is significant at p<0.001.

- identified health needs
- actions and services provided
- frequency and length of service
- person/agency responsible
- date service commenced
- planned outcomes
- date service ended
- actual outcomes.

The findings suggest an overall improvement in both the rate and quality of recording in relation to children's developmental needs. The changes were significant for the rate of recording identity and social presentation; and in relation to quality of recording, changes were significant for health, emotional and behavioural development, identity, and family and social relationships. With regard to parenting capacity and family and environmental factors the findings suggest that, although the rate of recording improved, the quality of the information remained largely unaffected (approximately half the information was categorised as completed well both before and after implementation of the Integrated Children's System; see Table 3.4).

Although better information was recorded on children's needs and circumstances this improvement did not apply to the summary of the review discussion or the reason for decision. For example the rate of recording the summary of the review discussion significantly decreased post implementation from being found on practically every case (97%) prior to implementation, to 61 per cent.[9] This may be due to the fact that prior to the introduction of the Integrated Children's System the decision and outcome of the conference was generally recorded in the minutes of the meeting. With the introduction of the Integrated Children's System the decisions and outcomes are recorded on the Child Protection Conference record. These are completed at the end of the conference to ensure those attending receive key information in writing as soon as possible after the conference.

---

9   t -tests for equality of means shows difference is significant at $p < 0.001$.

Discussion

Much of the feedback on the Integrated Children's System received by the research team concerned the child protection exemplars. Many practitioners commented that there was far more paperwork, too much information to record, and meetings and case conferences were taking much longer. However, the changes brought about with the implementation of the Integrated Children's System in relation to recording need to be understood.

Auditing social work case files prior to the implementation of the Integrated Children's System showed that, in general, far less information was recorded about children than about their parents or other relevant adults. The following case serves as an example. The record notes that the three children in this family had suffered serious neglect. The authorities intervened and the appropriate processes were put in place to protect the children, but in the subsequent assessments audited by the research team, a total of 15 words were recorded which related to the needs of these three children compared with far more information recorded about the parents. Admittedly, this was an extreme case, but the tendency to focus more on the needs and circumstances of the parents and other relevant adults, compared with children, was consistent across all authorities.

There is much research that shows the child's age, gender, birth position within the family and their relationships with members of the family and with peers are all factors that have an impact on a child's experience of abuse or neglect (Cleaver, Unell and Aldgate 1999; Dunn and McGuire 1992; Jones and Ramchandani 1999; Rutter 1985). The development of the Integrated Children's System was informed by legislation, research and good practice and the principle of considering children as individuals is at the heart of the system. However, it was clear from the child protection records that, prior to implementation, sibling groups were often considered together – the impact on individual children was not always addressed.

Before the introduction of the Integrated Children's System there was no specific format to ensure that information on some key child protection processes was recorded in a systematic and consistent way. As a result it was often difficult to locate a record of a strategy discussion or the outcome of a s47 enquiry, and when a record was found the quantity and quality of the information varied between cases.

The Integrated Children's System introduced major conceptual and practice changes to child protection processes and, although the training delivered by the research team to support implementation and the accompanying materials introduced practitioners to all aspects of the system, the time restraints prohibited any in-depth focus on child protection processes and recording practices. In addition, it was unlikely that during the early stages of implementation the processes and practical arrangements established within local authorities either sufficiently addressed or changed to take account of this new approach. The impact, therefore, was felt most keenly by practitioners in terms of the increase in paperwork and the time it took to prepare for meetings.

Nonetheless, despite the challenges facing social work practitioners, the findings suggest a trend towards an improvement in the quantity and quality of information recorded for child protection assessment, planning and reviews with the implementation of the Integrated Children's System. However, local authorities need to ensure that the summary of the review discussion and the reasons why decisions were taken are routinely recorded on the Child Protection Review report.

Findings: Children looked after (including those preparing for independence)

The part of the system which underwent the greatest change were the records relating to the looked after system. During the late 1990s, many social services departments across England and Wales had implemented part or all of the Looking After Children (LAC) system or some version of these materials. Some of the criticism to emerge from practitioners and managers about these materials concerned the link between the child's past before entering the looked after system, and the child's current circumstances. Children had often experienced changes in household and school, and were known to children's social care, but this historical information was not always captured consistently on the LAC forms when the child became looked after.

A further shortcoming to the LAC materials, identified by practitioners, was the difficulty in recording information about the parents' capacity to meet the needs of their child and the impact of wider family and environmental issues, particularly in cases where the plan was for the child to return home within a short period. In order to address such comments and to ensure the Integrated Children's System was integrated at this point of service delivery, the previous LAC records underwent radical change when incorporated into the Integrated Children's System.

Information gathering

One change that occurred with the introduction of the Integrated Children's System was the need to ensure that all children entering the looked after system had an updated or completed Referral and Information Record as the information from the LAC Essential Information Record had been incorporated into this record. Post implementation the scrutiny of case records showed that 58 per cent of looked after children had a Referral and Information Record on their files and 47 per cent had a completed Initial Assessment on file.

These figures should be seen in the context of local authorities' implementation timetable. Because the sample for the study included all children looked after at a particular date, a proportion of the children had become looked after prior to the implementation of the Integrated Children's System; no Referral and Information Record could have been completed. In implementing the Integrated Children's System local authorities adopted a step by step process; information on new cases or where significant events occurred was recorded using the new system. Introducing the Referral and Information Record for children who had been looked after for some time where placements were stable was being rolled out more gradually.

The Chronology was designed to ensure that information in relation to significant events in children's lives was consistently and systematically recorded for all children in need, and not only those looked after. For looked after children it ensures that information about significant events, which occurred before they became looked after, is recorded, allowing subsequent decisions and actions to be placed in context. The Chronology replaces the Essential Information Record Part 2.

> The Chronology collects salient information on key events and changes in relation to a child/young person. It has been developed in response to widespread recognition by practitioners of the need to identify patterns and relationships between events in a child's life. (*ibid.*, Briefing Paper No.5, p.3)

The Chronology contained within the Integrated Children's System covers seven areas and provides a record of:

- social services activity
- child's health history
- education, training and employment history
- changes in the child's legal status

- placement history for looked after children
- history of any offences
- significant events and changes in the child/young person's birth family and wider social networks.

As such the Chronology exemplar provides a specification for the areas that a Chronology should cover and the minimum information that should be recorded in each of these areas.

The study compared the information recorded on 62 Essential Information Records completed pre implementation with 56 Chronologies post implementation. The findings show that the change from the Essential Information Record Part 2 to the Chronology had a mixed impact on recording practice. For example, recording children's services' activity increased from 37 per cent to 86 per cent. However, there was little impact on the recording of a child's placement history (71% to 75%) or the birth family and wider networks (24% to 29%). In contrast, the recording of the child's education and health history decreased significantly from 75 per cent for both to 21 per cent[10] and 34 per cent[11] respectively, resulting in gaps in the essential information about a child's life. The decrease in recording was not associated with the identity of the local authority.

A factor which may have affected whether information on the child's education and health history was found on the Chronology was the timing of its implementation. The Chronology is designed to be populated from other exemplars, particularly the Review, but at the time of the study the pilot authorities' IT systems did not yet have this level of functionality. As a result, practitioners needed to re-record the child's education and health history directly onto the Chronology.

The Placement Information Record was designed to replace the Placement Plan. It is completed at the time a child becomes looked after. It contains key information required by carers in order to provide appropriate care for an individual child and the parental agreements to:

- a period of accommodation under s20
- specified medical treatments

---

10   t -tests for equality of means shows difference is significant at p<0.001.

11   t -tests for equality of means shows difference is significant at p<0.001.

- delegation of a number of responsibilities, including, for example, consent to overnight stays

- contact arrangements. (*ibid.*, Briefing Paper No.5, p.3)

The information recorded on 57 Placement Plans pre implementation was compared with that recorded on 49 Placement Information Records post implementation. The findings suggest this change has had little effect on recording practice.

The reason for placement and the type of placement were recorded by all three authorities in practically every case both before and after implementation. Similarly, recording information about a child's routines continued to be regularly noted (found on 82 per cent of cases pre implementation and on 90 per cent of cases post implementation). However, scant attention continued to be given to recording the child's emotional and behavioural development, noted on 42 per cent of cases before implementation, and 46 per cent after implementation.

Information about the child's health was recorded on most Placement Plans and their replacement, the Placement Information Records for looked after children. An analysis of these data suggests that specific medical assessments for looked after children are not routinely carried out, a practice that has not been affected by the implementation of the Integrated Children's System. Less than half the children and young people (43.8%) had the advantage of a pre-placement medical prior to the Integrated Children's System, a figure that fell to just over a third (35%) for medical assessments since the implementation.

The Integrated Children's System resulted in an increase in the recording of key information about the arrangements to meet the child's educational needs. For example, whether a child or young person had a Personal Education Plan was more likely to be recorded (found on 79 per cent of Placement Information Records) since the implementation of the Integrated Children's System than before implementation (found on 54 per cent of the Placement Plans). Recording the name and address of the school or pre-school provision remained high, noted on approximately three-quarters of relevant cases both before and after implementation.

Closure Records

The Closure Record summarises the impact of actions and services provided to a child and family, and the evidence that supports the decision to close a case. (*ibid.*, Briefing Paper No.5, p.4)

As the audit was designed to focus on open cases it was not possible to scrutinise Closure Records.

Assessment

The majority of children who become looked after have complex needs and have been in receipt of services from children's social care for some time. As a consequence, in many cases an up-to-date core assessment may have been available at the point of entry to the looked after system prior to the implementation of the Integrated Children's System.

CORE ASSESSMENT RECORD

One of the key changes to the looked after system was that all children entering care should have an up-to-date core assessment.

> When a child becomes looked after, an up-to-date core assessment is required and is used to inform the child's first Care Plan. (*ibid.*, Briefing Paper No.5, p.4)

A current core assessment of the child and their family will ensure appropriate services and supports are put in place, particularly if the plan is for the child to return home in the short term. Moreover, the information recorded in the Core Assessment Record about the child's needs will provide a baseline from which progress and the impact of services can be measured.

The findings show that, prior to the implementation of the Integrated Children's System, seven looked after children had a completed core assessment on their files. Post implementation this increased to 19, accounting for 50 per cent of the looked after cases audited. The findings suggest that the Integrated Children's System is beginning to change practice.

ASSESSMENT AND PROGRESS RECORD

> The Assessment and Progress Records are used to assess and monitor the developmental progress of looked after children, and to inform the Care Plan. The first Assessment and Progress Record builds on the information in the Core Assessment Record.

> A decision to complete an Assessment and Progress Record is made at the second review, i.e. at four months from the start of the current care episode. This Record is to be completed by the time of the third review, i.e. at ten months from the start of the current care episode. There are four age related Assessment and Progress Records: 1–2, 3–4, 5–10 and 11–15 years. (*ibid.*, Briefing Paper No.5, p.5)

The Assessment and Progress Record within the Integrated Children's System was developed to provide an in-depth assessment of a looked after child's progress. Previous research suggests that insufficient attention is given to monitoring the progress of children looked after (Moyers 1997; Peel 1998; Scott 1999). The finding from this research showed that in the first year of being looked after only 40 per cent of assessments were completed for children for whom a decision had been made for them to remain within the looked after system in the long term. This figure declined to approximately 9 per cent for subsequent assessments (Scott 2000).

The findings from the current study suggest that the Integrated Children's System has made little impact on the failure to monitor routinely the progress of children looked after over time. Only 11 Assessment and Action Records were found on the 36 children looked after included in the first audit, and, although completed Assessment and Progress Records were not expected on case files post implementation, no records (regardless of their stage of completion) were found.

Planning

A key change introduced by the Integrated Children's System was separating the Care Plan for looked after children into two parts. Part 1 sets out the overall aim of the plan for the child and Part 2 identifies the services and actions required to respond to the child's identified developmental needs. The aim of the change was to ensure that the plan for the child was relevant and identified not simply the overall objective but the specific actions and services required to achieve these in order to meet the child's needs. A key finding from inspections and previous research, confirmed in this study, is that Care Plans for children are often out of date and not located on the child's current file (Scott 2000; Social Services Inspectorate 1999). When a child is receiving respite care it would not be necessary to complete Part 2 of the Care Plan if a current Child's Plan (the result of a core assessment) is already in place.

With the implementation of the Integrated Children's System, Care Plans for different groups of children and young people were harmonised. The Adoption Plan replaces Part 2 of the Care Plan where a decision has been made that adoption is the most appropriate plan for permanence; it outlines the key processes and timescales. For young people preparing for independence the Pathway Plan replaces Part 2 of the Care Plan.

CARE PLANS FOR LOOKED AFTER CHILDREN

The impact of the Integrated Children's System on care planning is based on a scrutiny of 63 Care Plans for looked after children prior to implementation and 51 post implementation. The findings suggest that the Integrated Children's System affected aspects of recording Care Plans differentially.

Some parts of the Care Plan were unaffected and the rate of recording remained high. For example, when children became looked after all three local authorities recorded key information, such as the child's current legal status, reason for the child/young person being looked after, and the overall or chosen Care Plan, in practically every case both before and after implementation of the Integrated Children's System.

Other aspects of the Care Plan, although showing an increase in the rate of recording, remained low. For example, recording whether a Personal Education Assessment had been completed increased overall from 39 per cent to 54 per cent, as did recording information on whether a Personal Health Assessment had been completed from 34 per cent to 45 per cent by the second audit.

The trend for improved recording also applied to information about the child's developmental needs. A comparison of the Care Plans pre and post implementation shows that the rate of recording information about the child's developmental needs remained high with a general trend towards improvement, as Table 3.5 illustrates.

Of more significance was the finding that the quality of recording had improved ('completed well' referred to plans where information was recorded under each heading in each table for a particular developmental need). The data show a substantial improvement in the quality of information recorded for every developmental dimension, of which all except the child's education and family and social relationships were found to be at least statistically significant at $p<0.001$.

The Integrated Children's System ensures that Part 2 of the Care Plan covers the birth family and corporate parenting (corporate parenting refers to the local authority including those responsible for the day-to-day care of the child), issues not generally explored in Care Plans prior to implementation. As a result no comparison in the rate of recording was possible. A scrutiny of the Care Plans post implementation suggests information was more likely to be recorded about birth parents than corporate parents. For example, in relation to birth parents, information on their parenting capacity had been recorded in over three-quarters of cases (79%) and family and environmental factors in 64

Table 3.5 Information recorded on Care Plans

	Audit 1 (n=63)	Audit 2 (n=51)
Child's development needs		
Health	77%, of which 48% completed well	82%, of which 84% completed well
Education	81%, of which 41% completed well	77%, of which 73% completed well
Emotional and behavioural development	52%, of which 24% completed well	87%, of which 62% completed well
Identity	71%, of which 36% completed well	79%, of which 77% completed well
Family and social relationships	73%, of which 41% completed well	87%, of which 71% completed well
Social presentation	41%, of which 12% completed well	64%, of which 84% completed well
Self-care skills	43%, of which 11% completed well	64%, of which 88% completed well

per cent of cases. In comparison both these issues in relation to corporate parenting had been noted in approximately half the cases. However, when examining the quality of the information the reverse was true; when information was noted about corporate parenting this was more detailed than information relating to birth parenting.

The rate of recording information on parenting capacity and family and environmental factors was related to the identity of the authority. Information on these domains was recorded in over three-quarters of cases (79% for birth parents and 86% for corporate parents) in the Welsh Local Authority, not quite so consistently in the Shire County (50% and 69% respectively) and less well in the London Borough (44% and 22% respectively).

Previous research from the mid-1990s highlighted the dearth of review forms found on the case files for looked after children (Grimshaw and Sinclair 1997). However, following implementation of Looking After Children in the late 1990s, reviewing looked after children was one area where processes were becoming established and the completion of review documents were more consistent (Moyers 1997; Peel 1998; Scott 1999).

The findings from the implementation of the Integrated Children's System suggest that the attention given to forthcoming reviews at the planning stage has continued. For example, establishing and recording the date of the review is the first step to ensuring the process takes place. Prior to the Integrated Children's System the review date had been noted on 44 per cent of Care Plans while post Integrated Children's System this information was found on 73 per cent of Care Plans.

ADOPTION PLANS

As only one Adoption Plan had been completed, no conclusions could be drawn from this.

PATHWAY PLANS

In exploring the impact of the Integrated Children's System on recording Pathway Plans, 21 plans completed prior to implementation were compared with 17 post implementation Pathway Plans.

The Pathway Plan fulfils the requirements both for assessing the young person's needs and planning services. It is divided into two parts. The first part records the assessed needs of the young person. Part 2 sets out the services that are required to respond to the identified needs and to provide support during the transition to adulthood (see Briefing Paper 5, Department of Health and Department for Education and Skills 2000–2005).

The scrutiny of case records shows a consistently high rate of recording some aspects on the assessment. For example, information about the young person's health, education, self-care and social presentation, financial needs and accommodation was noted in practically all cases both before and after implementation (see Table 3.6).

Of particular importance is the marked improvement that the Integrated Children's System has had on the rate of recording other aspects of young people's needs. For example, before implementation information on the young person's family and social relationships was noted on only 33 per cent of Pathway Plans and information on their emotional and behavioural development on 24 per cent of Plans. After implementation the rate increased to 94 per cent for both issues, a change that was significant for both dimensions (see Table 3.6).

Table 3.6 Information recorded on Pathway Plans

	Part 1: Assessment		Part 2: Plan	
	Audit 1 (n=21)	Audit 2 (n=17)	Audit 1 (n=21)	Audit 2 (n=17)
Health needs	100%, of which 57% completed well	94%, of which 88% completed well	95%, of which 35% specific	71%, of which 58% specific
Education/ training needs	95%, of which 60% completed well	94%, of which 94% completed well	100%, of which 47% specific	76%, of which 69% specific
Identity needs	81%, of which 29% completed well	94%, of which 94% completed well	90%, of which 37% specific	71%, of which 25% specific
Family and social relationship needs	33%, of which 43% completed well	94%, of which 94% completed well	76%, of which 25% specific	71%, of which 42% specific
Emotional and behavioural needs	24%, of which 40% completed well	94%, of which 94% completed well	66%, of which 14% specific	77%, of which 62% specific
Self-care and social presentation needs	90%, of which 47% completed well	94%, of which 94% completed well	95%, of which 35% specific	75%, of which 50% specific
Finance needs	86%, of which 44% completed well	94%, of which 75% completed well	86%, of which 39% specific	69%, of which 64% specific
Support	90%, of which 47% completed well	82%, of which 71% completed well	95%, of which 50% specific	81%, of which 62% specific
Accommoda-tion needs	90%, of which 21% completed well	94%, of which 81% completed well	100%, of which 62% specific	75%, of which 58% specific

The trend towards improvements in recording also applied to the quality of recording; improvements were identified for every dimension with the change being significant in relation to: identity, family and social relationships, emotional and behavioural development, self-care and social presentation, and accommodation (see Table 3.6).

The findings also suggest that the Integrated Children's System has increased the likelihood of social work practitioners to record an analysis of young people's needs. For example, prior to the implementation of the Integrated Children's System an analysis of needs was found in 29 per cent of Pathway Plans – this rose to two-thirds of cases (65%) post implementation. Although this should be welcomed, a more detailed scrutiny of the analysis suggests there is no room for complacency. In only a third of cases (both before and after implementation of the Integrated Children's System) did the analysis identify the most appropriate service.

The identified trend towards improved Pathway Plans was also apparent from the scrutiny of Part 2 of the Plan. The findings suggest that, although the Integrated Children's System had little effect on the rate of recording, remaining relatively high, improvements were identified with regard to specificity of the Plan (to be rated as specific, information had to have been recorded on the arrangements to put in place, the person or agency responsible, and the timescales). For example, although increases in the specificity of Plans to meet young people's needs were apparent for practically every area of development, the greatest improvement was in relation to emotional and behavioural development; before the Integrated Children's System 14 per cent of Plans were specific, a figure that rose to 62 per cent post Integrated Children's System (see Table 3.6).

Government Regulations and Guidance (Department of Health 2001a) stresses the importance of practitioners anticipating potential crises in the lives of young people leaving care, and building contingency arrangements into the Pathway Plans. The findings show that a lack of recorded contingency planning was a feature in social work records both before and after the implementation of the Integrated Children's System. For example, only 6 of the 20 young people's Pathway Plans (30%) recorded pre implementation contained a specific contingency plan for any area of their lives. Post implementation the rate remained low; only 3 of the 18 Pathway Plans (16.6%) contained any specific contingency plans. Although the numbers are too small to draw any conclusions, nonetheless the findings suggest that at present contingency planning is unspecific and simply identifies that an alternative action or service may be required. Contingency plans rarely identified the type of service or how it was to be provided.

Reviewing

THE REVIEW RECORD

> The Review Record is intended for use in all reviews of children in need. It is used to review the Child's Plan, the Child Protection Plan, the Care Plan and the Pathway Plan in accordance with time-scales laid down in regulations and guidance. (*ibid.*, Briefing Paper No.5, p.6)

The Integrated Children's System Review Record was designed to review the specific information recorded on the plan for the child. Within an IT system the information from the current plan would pre-populate the review record.

REVIEW RECORD FOR CHILDREN LOOKED AFTER

To identify the impact of the Integrated Children's System on reviews for looked after children, 70 reviews prior to implementation were compared with 64 post implementation.

The findings suggest that the Integrated Children's System has had a mixed impact on the quantity and quality of information recorded on Review Records for looked after children and young people. For example, although the rate and quality of recording has decreased somewhat in relation to five of the seven developmental dimensions, the findings suggest greater attention is being given to the child or young person's social presentation and their self-care skills post implementation (see Table 3.7).

Reviewing parenting capacity and family and environmental factors was introduced with the Integrated Children's System and as a result no comparison of recording could be made. A scrutiny of the Review Record for looked after children post implementation suggests that reviews were more likely to include information about the birth family than the corporate parent (mirroring the findings for Care Plans). For example, information about the birth family's parenting capacity was found in 70 per cent of cases, but only 59 per cent of cases recorded details about the corporate parents' capacity. Similarly, the amount of information available about the child's own wider family and environment was recorded in 70 per cent of cases, but only 53 per cent of cases recorded information about the environmental factors relating to the corporate parent.

Table 3.7 Information recorded about a child's developmental needs on Looked After Reviews

	Audit 1 (n=70)	Audit (n=64)
Child's development needs		
Health	100%, of which 83% completed well (n=69)	94%, of which 73% completed well (n=64)
Education	97%, of which 78% completed well (n=64)	88%, of which 61% completed well (n=57)
Emotional and behavioural development	86%, of which 66% completed well (n=69)	81%, of which 56% completed well (n=64)
Identity	93%, of which 66% completed well (n=70)	80%, of which 53% completed well (n=64)
Family and social relationships	94%, of which 71% completed well (n=70)	89%, of which 54% completed well (n=64)
Social presentation	66%, of which 46% completed well (n=70)	80%, of which 65% completed well (n=64)
Self-care skills	60%, of which 57% completed well (n=70)	80%, of which 67% completed well (n=64)

The n figures differ because information was not recorded for every dimension.

Information within the Review Record about the current care plan and current placement were routinely recorded in all authorities both prior to and after the introduction of the Integrated Children's System. For example, the current care plan was recorded in 97 per cent of cases pre implementation and details on the current placement were recorded in 94 per cent of cases. Post implementation the number of cases where this information had been recorded, although slightly reduced, remained high (89% and 84% respectively).

Where it was applicable, the rate of recording whether children and young people had been consulted about their review increased from 63 per cent to 85 per cent, of which about half attended their reviews. The rate of recording the review discussion showed little change; it was found in 84 per cent of cases before implementation and 78 per cent post implementation.

Discussion

The impact of the Integrated Children's System on recording information on looked after children has been mixed. The rate of recording on information-gathering records, such as the Chronology, varies with some data being more consistently noted, such as the history of children's social care activity, while recording information on other aspects of the child's life, such as their health and education history, declined.

A number of factors had an impact on the use of the Chronology. For example, there was an ongoing debate between practitioners and IT consultants as to the purpose of a chronology. IT experts saw it as an output of all the information already held within an organisation's database, while practitioners wanted it to be a tool to gather and record key information about a child's life. This continuing debate led authorities to take different approaches in its implementation, some using it as an output providing a record of all activity on a particular issue held on existing exemplars within the Integrated Children's System, while others implemented it as a tool for practitioners to record information. However, using the Chronology as an output is not straightforward because, although much of the necessary information can be drawn from existing records, some information is not recorded on existing exemplar records, such as that relating to a child's health and education history. As a result this information must be either entered directly onto the record or recorded specifically into the system so that it is available to pull from the database into the Chronology. These difficulties are reflected in the finding that, at the point of the fieldwork, all the pilots were continuing to develop their chronology-building facilities (see Chapter 7).

Perhaps the greatest barrier to the use of the Chronology was that, at the time of the study, children's social care and the courts required different chronologies of key events in the life of a child. The seven headings under which information is gathered in the present Chronology were developed for use by children's social care; to meet the requirements of the courts information must be organised under different headings. Work, to resolve the differences, is being taken forward by the Department for Children, Schools and Families. In the light of this some pilots chose to delay fully implementing the Chronology.

Assessment continues to be an issue for looked after children. Although an up-to-date core assessment on children who became looked after was considered good practice prior to the Integrated Children's System, making it a requirement has resulted in comprehensive baseline information about children's needs being available for a greater proportion of children entering the care system.

It was not expected that all looked after children would have either an Assessment and Action Record or its replacement, the Assessment and Progress Record, on their case file. For example, some children were newly looked after and it was too early to complete a long-term assessment, and for others, the plan was to return home in the short term. Furthermore, for two authorities, the audit took place before the Integrated Children's System was in place for a year or more and the process of implementation was still under way. Nevertheless, it is of concern that only 11 Assessment and Action Records were found in the first audit and no Assessment and Progress Records were completed by the time of the second. The findings suggest that no consistent and regular assessment of the progress of children who have such severe needs that they have to be looked after by the state continues and the implementation of the Integrated Children's System has yet to have an impact on practice.

Another area of practice which changed with the implementation of the Integrated Children's System was the Pathway Plan. Although the planning part of the process was evident in the records both before and after implementation, there was more evidence of young people's needs being assessed once the system was in place. Prior to implementation the relationship between assessment and planning was less clear and it was not always apparent what assessments were being undertaken to inform the arrangements and plans for young people preparing to leave care. Post implementation, the relationship between the young person's assessment of needs and the plan developed to meet those needs was far more explicit.

Both before and after implementation, plans for young people preparing for independence considered the health, education, employment or training, finance, accommodation and support in place for the young person. However, prior to implementation, the young person's family and social relationships, and emotional and behavioural development, were rarely addressed in the plan, despite findings from research that isolation and mental health are key factors associated with successful transition to independence (Marsh and Peel 1999; Stein 2004). The findings from the present study suggest that the Integrated Children's System is affecting practice; both these issues were more explicitly addressed in case records completed post implementation.

The findings suggest that there has been a mixed impact on the recording of reviews for looked after children. The interviews with practitioners and managers responsible for reviewing the needs of children looked after provide some insight. For example, review chairs have welcomed the changes because they have increased the emphasis on outcomes and support a more child-centred approach. However, practitioners report that the changes between the formats of existing records and those introduced with the Integrated Children's System made it difficult to locate and record information, resulting in the process taking longer. This problem should be resolved with greater familiarity with the system.

Summary points

- The impact of the Integrated Children's System on social work recording was assessed through auditing social work case files in three local authorities before implementation and at least six months after.

- The timing of implementation affected the findings; when practitioners have to learn new processes and systems, practice temporarily deteriorates.

- The Integrated Children's System brings few changes to the Referral and Information Record. Nonetheless, substantial improvements were found in relation to recording (a) parental awareness of a referral and (b) the outcome of the referral. Post implementation this information was recorded in the majority of cases.

- The Integrated Children's System introduces a plan to the initial assessment. A plan was found in less than half of initial assessments (45%) following the implementation, suggesting this had not yet become established practice.

- The Integrated Children's System separates the child's plan from the core assessment. Although significantly more information is being recorded on the child's plan, the quality of recording parenting capacity and family and environmental factors needs to be given greater attention.

- The Integrated Children's System replaces and introduces new records for children in need of protection which focus on individual children rather than sibling groups. The findings indicate that the newly introduced Record of Strategy Discussion and the Record of Outcome of s47 Enquiries are both being used comprehensively.

- The recording of Initial Child Protection Conference Reports has improved. Of particular significance is the improvement to the quality of the analysis; 13 per cent of the analysis was classed as detailed prior to implementation while 67 per cent was so classed post implementation.

- The impact on recording of Child Protection Reviews has been mixed. While information on children's developmental needs, parenting capacity and family and environmental factors increased, recording the summary of the review discussion and the reason for the decision decreased.

- The Chronology in the Integrated Children's System replaces the Essential Information Record Part 2 for children looked after. This change has had a mixed impact; recording social services' activity improved, while recording the child's education and health history declined.

- The Placement Information Record replaces the Placement Plan for children looked after, and the impact on recording is varied. Some issues were not affected, such as recording the reason and type of placement, which was found on practically every case both before and after implementation. However, recording information about the child's health was less well completed post implementation, while recording the arrangements to meet the child's educational needs increased.

- With the Integrated Children's System all children entering the care system should have an up-to-date core assessment. The findings show practice is changing; a core assessment was found in half the cases. However, the Integrated Children's System has made little impact on the endemic failure to monitor routinely the progress of children looked after; no Assessment and Progress Records were found on the case files post implementation.

- The Care Plan has been separated into two parts. Part 1 covers the assessment of the child's needs and applies to all looked after children while Part 2 identifies the services and actions needed to respond to these needs. When appropriate the Adoption Plan and the Pathway Plan replaces Part 2 of the Care Plan. The birth parent and corporate parenting are included.

- Some aspects of the Care Plan are unaffected and recording remained high, for example the legal status of the child, reason for care, and chosen care plan. Whether the young person had a

Personal Education Assessment or Personal Health Plan continued to be noted in approximately half the cases. Other aspects of recording improved, in particular the quality of recording children's needs. Information was more likely to be recorded about birth parents than corporate parenting.

- In general the implementation of the Integrated Children's System improved the recording of the Pathway Plan. Information was more likely to be recorded on Part 1 and Part 2 of the Pathway Plan. Moreover, the quality of much of the recording improved significantly.

- The Integrated Children's System has introduced birth parents and corporate parents into the review process. The impact has been mixed and reflects that found for Care Plans; information relating to birth parents is more likely to be covered in the review than corporate parenting.

Chapter 4

Impact on Recording –
Social Workers' Perceptions

Introduction

> The Integrated Children's System will provide an assessment, planning, intervention and reviewing model for all children in need under the Children Act 1989. (Department of Health and Department for Education and Skills 2000–2005, Briefing Paper No.1)

Local authorities are responsible for promoting and safeguarding the welfare of children in need and as a result the Integrated Children's System had the greatest impact on the work of managers and practitioners within children's social care. To explore how the changes were experienced information was drawn from the questionnaires completed by 52 social work practitioners who attended the research workshops. In addition, information from 46 postal questionnaires completed by social work practitioners provided insights into their attitudes and use of IT (see Appendix 1 for details).

Any difficulties that local authorities encountered need to be carefully considered and this chapter attempts to distinguish between issues caused by the introduction of the Integrated Children's System and issues caused by IT systems (both those that resulted generally from the move from paper to electronic records and those caused by an authority's particular IT system).

Profile of the social workers

Social workers' knowledge base and confidence in using the Integrated Children's System may be affected by whether, and for how long, they have been qualified (Cleaver *et al.* 2004b). The Integrated Children's System is predicated on social workers having a sound knowledge of child development, the factors that influence parenting capacity, and the ways wider family and environmental factors can affect children and their families. Practitioners in children's social care will need to apply this conceptual model to all their work with children irrespective of their circumstances.

The social workers who commented on the Integrated Children's System had a range of work experience. For example, 3 had no professional qualification, approximately a quarter (28%) had been qualified for less than three years, whereas over half (54%) had been qualified for ten years or more.

It could be argued that the length of time practitioners and managers have worked within their present agency will affect the way they react to change. For example, perceptions will be influenced by the informal and formal cultures within the agency, and by their knowledge of protocols, procedures and guidance. The group of practitioners who reported their experiences of the Integrated Children's System were as likely to have worked in their current agency for less than three years (44.2%) as they were to have worked there for ten years or more (44.2%).

Once fully implemented the Integrated Children's System will impact on all children in contact with children's social care, regardless of their circumstances. The experience of social workers involved in the study enabled them to report on how it had affected work with children in different circumstances. For example, two-thirds (66%) of the group reported that they routinely (at least once a week) worked with children in need of protection, practically three-quarters (73%) with children looked after, just over a third (36%) with young people leaving care, 12 per cent with children in adoption proceedings, and 89 per cent with other groups of children.

Training on the Integrated Children's System

Previous research on implementing new ways of working with children and families suggests that staff training is an essential element to changing practice (see, for example, Cleaver and Nicholson 2005; Cleaver *et al.* 2004a; Ward 1995b). However, at the time of the research, less than half (44%) the social workers reported attending any in-house training on the Integrated Children's System; 18 per cent attended multi-agency training.

Insufficient training was an issue highlighted by many social work managers and practitioners as hindering their understanding of the system and their ability to use it effectively.

> Lack of training prior to implementation of ICS was a major failing. The Integrated Children's System documents are not working documents that are easily understood by social workers, children and families. (Welsh Local Authority, manager)

> I feel the Integrated Children's System is a good system in principle for improving assessment to planning, but staff have not been trained in its implementation and therefore the quality has not improved – in fact, it decreases for new workers until they have absorbed on the job training and with a high turnover of staff this is quite a problem. (London Borough, manager)

The provision of training was related to the identity of the local authority and reflects how far they had progressed in their implementation programme. It will be recalled from Chapter 2 that the Welsh Local Authority developed its Integrated Children's System IT system in-house and experienced fewer difficulties. In addition, this authority initially utilised its existing administration staff to undertake all direct data entry, thus allowing practitioners to concentrate on understanding the impact of the Integrated Children's System on practice. Their implementation had two clear prongs, an IT development and a change in practice – training, both in-house and multi-agency, was supplied to address both issues.

The results from the Welsh Local Authority were encouraging; over half the staff (55.8%) in this authority reported attending either intra- or inter-agency training compared with 38.9 per cent in the Shire County and 12.5 per cent in the London Borough where time to train staff had been restricted due to their need to introduce a new IT system (see Chapter 2 for details).

The impact on recording practice

The findings indicate that the impact of the Integrated Children's System on social work recording is significant; approximately three-quarters of social workers (78.4%) reported their practice had changed as a result of the Integrated Children's System. Nonetheless, this suggests that practically a quarter did not think their recording practice had been affected. An exploration of the data suggests the characteristics of the practitioners were not relevant. No association was found between the perceptions of social workers and training, the focus of their work (for example, children in need, or children looked after), the length of time since qualifying, or their status (managers or practitioners).

However, social workers who thought their recording practice had not changed were clustered in two authorities, suggesting that the method of implementation may have been influential. The first was the Welsh Local Authority where administrative staff had been initially responsible for recording data on their new electronic system and the second was the Shire County where implementation had been done area by area and at the time of the data collection the Integrated Children's System had not been fully rolled out.

Changes to recording assessment and reports

The Integrated Children's System has resulted in major changes to the way professionals working in children's social care record information about children and their families. Changes relate to all aspects of work including changes to assessments – initial, core and pathway; changes to plans – initial, child protection and pathway; changes to reviews – looked after children review; and changes in reports – child protection and chairs' reports. These fundamental changes are reflected in the reports of practitioners and managers.

> Most reports we write are now different. (Welsh Local Authority, practitioner)

> As part of social services our work has been directly changed by the ICS and we now use ICS formats for most if not all our reports. (Welsh Local Authority, practitioner)

Changes were identified both in terms of the amount of information now recorded and its quality (reflecting the findings from the audit of case records discussed in the previous chapter). For example, two-thirds of practitioners and managers (65.9%) reported that the quantity of recorded information had increased. An increase in social work recording was to be expected because the Integrated Children's System requires practitioners to record, for example, information on individual children not families, to carry out and record reviews of children in need, and to carry out and record more comprehensive Pathway Plans for children looked after. These changes ensure that social work practice conforms to child care legislation and government guidance (Children Act 1989; Department of Health *et al.* 2000a).

An increase in recording, however, may not reflect improvements in practice. IT systems which do not allow information to populate from one record to another can result in information having to be re-entered and cause practitioners to become frustrated and disillusioned with the system.

> LAC information is more lengthy, repetitive and computerised. Makes it difficult to meet the timescales set by government. (Shire County, practitioner)

> Lots of repetition and duplication of information required on forms. Clarification is needed (possibly training) to identify what specific information is required under relevant heading to hopefully reduce repetition. (Welsh Local Authority, practitioner)

Twelve practitioners and one manager thought the amount of information recorded about children and families had either remained the same (n=9) or decreased (n=4). The findings suggest that the method of implementation may influence this perception. Five of those who perceived no change, and all 4 of those who thought less information was now recorded, worked in the Welsh Local Authority where administrative staff initially entered information on the data-base. This group were primarily social work practitioners (8 of the 9) and accounted for practically all the practitioners from this authority (8 of 10). The intention in this authority is, once the IT system is glitch free, for social workers to take over the responsibility for entering case information directly onto the data-base. Once this happens it would be expected that practitioners will experience an increase in their workloads.

Perceptions were more mixed on whether the quality of the information recorded on children and families had improved with the introduction of the Integrated Children's System. A similar proportion of the group thought that quality had improved (28.2%) as thought that it had deteriorated (30.8%); the remaining 41 per cent considered it had not changed. For example, some managers and practitioners found the system resulted in more focused record keeping.

> More outcome focused; clearly identifies roles and responsibilities, timescales, service deficiencies, shortfall. (Welsh Local Authority, practitioner)

> The assessments, reports and audits are less narrative in format and contain more focused tasks or plans. (Welsh Local Authority, manager)

For managers, the improved quality of social work recording and the introduction of an electronic recording system enabled them to carry out their own role more effectively.

> ICS has made the task of undertaking file audits less time consuming as plans are, in most cases, clearly laid-out. (Welsh Local Authority, manager)

However, a common complaint voiced by practitioners when considering the impact of the Integrated Children's System on the quality of social work practice was that the formats used for assessments, plans and reports were not family friendly.

> The system appears to be unfair to families when trying to explain the plan to them. The system produces so much information and paper that families are disempowered by it all. (Welsh Local Authority, practitioner)

> The ICS documents are not working documents that are easily understood by social workers, children and families. (Welsh Local Authority, practitioner)

> Brilliant idea as a concept, but exemplars not service user friendly. (London Borough, practitioner)

These remarks relate to four issues raised by social work practitioners:

- The language and terminology used in the exemplars, for example 'social presentation' and 'corporate parenting capacity', were thought to be difficult for some children and families to understand.

- The size of formats, in particular the Core Assessment and Assessment and Progress Records, was felt to be overwhelming for some children and families.

- The change from family to child focused reports, for example in child protection cases, resulted in parents receiving several reports which often repeated information, such as issues affecting parenting capacity.

- The format used for some records, in particular the plan, was met with a mixed response. While some practitioners thought it confused children and families, others reported that its specificity made it easier to follow. The different views may reflect the way IT systems produce the 'outputs' of the plan. Initially some IT systems printed all pages of a record, regardless of whether they contained any information. As a result some parents received large, bulky documents, much of which was blank.

The concerns that the formats are not family friendly reflect the purpose of the exemplars, in that they were developed as professional tools to support the recording of information relevant to a child's needs and circumstances. They were not designed as tools for direct work with children and families.

Practitioners must use their professional skills and judgement to obtain the necessary information, which is then recorded in the authority's IT system. However, once the information is in the data base it can be manipulated in a variety of ways to produce 'outputs' or records for children and families. For example, previous research found that many parents only wanted a copy of the summary, analysis and planning sections of the Core Assessment, which were in written format and provided them with the conclusion and outcome of the assessment (Cleaver *et al.* 2004b).

The timescale of the current research meant that there was limited opportunity for authorities to review the way in which they output information for families. All authorities had changed or were in the process of changing the way in which records were printed to ensure that only completed sections were produced. In addition the Welsh Local Authority did change the order of the information contained in the plans and review record to make them more 'user friendly'.

There was also discussion amongst some practitioners across all the pilot authorities of the possibility of developing more child and family friendly explanations for some of the concepts used within the Integrated Children's System. The challenge for authorities is to produce outputs which are user friendly without developing two sets of records, one of which is unavailable to families.

Impact on the use of IT

The perceived amount of IT work associated with the Integrated Children's System will depend on a number of factors including the provision of computer hardware, the general IT skills of the practitioners, and how easy the Integrated Children's System software is to use.

Use of IT prior to the implementation of the Integrated Children's System

Forty-six social work practitioners completed a questionnaire on their use of IT in the workplace. The findings suggest that the level of IT competence amongst practitioners prior to the implementation of the Integrated Children's System was generally good and practically all reported having ready access to a computer. For example, most practitioners (89%) stated that before implementation they used a computer at work on at least a weekly basis and felt comfortable in using IT, a finding at variance to the widely held stereotype that significant numbers of social workers have few IT skills. Practitioners reported that they most frequently used IT, before the introduction of the Integrated Children's System, to send and receive email (91%), for word processing (69%) and to write case notes (64%).

Use of IT after the implementation of the Integrated Children's System

Although social workers use computers for much of their day-to-day work, the implementation of the Integrated Children's System means that all assessments, records and reports on children and families must be electronic. Moreover, it is a system that enables managers and social workers to more readily access information on individual children and groups of children.

> The flow of information has improved and access to information pertaining to a particular child is easier to access even if you don't work in the same team. (London Borough, Children's social care)

As would be expected, the implementation of the Integrated Children's System led to an increase in the amount of work done using IT; 61 per cent of practitioners reported that they were using IT more. Not only was there an increase in the overall time spent using IT but, more significantly, a change in the purpose for which it was used. For example, since the implementation of the Integrated Children's System practitioners reported spending rather less time word processing and dealing with emails, but considerably more time accessing information on individual children and groups of children (see Table 4.1).

The data shown in Table 4.1 suggest a shift away from using IT to simply carry out administrative functions to using it as a tool to access and aggregate data to manage work more effectively.

Practitioners also reported having to spend more time in keying in information about children and families. Some practitioners saw this as a barrier to therapeutic work, and a significant proportion (42.1%) used it as little as possible, believing IT impacted negatively on their work with children and families. This echoes previous findings in relation to recording more generally which was viewed by many practitioners as an administrative rather than practice task (Kagle 1993). However, their explanatory comments suggest that the increase in time spent inputting data may have owed much to unresolved problems with IT systems, particularly issues in relation to single data entry, and practitioners' unfamiliarity with using new systems. Although practitioners resented the additional time spent at the computer, almost all of them (98%) accepted the importance and usefulness of IT in their daily practice.

**Table 4.1 Practitioners' reports of IT tasks performed
at least once per week**

Task	Prior to implementation		Post implementation		Change
Word process	31	69%	29	64%	–4%
Key in data	23	51%	32	71%	20%
Access info on individual children	17	38%	39	87%	49%
Access info on groups of children	7	16%	15	33%	18%
E-mail	41	91%	40	89%	–2%
Diary functions	13	29%	16	36%	7%
Access inter/intranet	26	58%	27	60%	2%
Write case notes	29	64%	31	69%	4%
Other	20	44%	20	44%	0%
n=45					

IT training

For practitioners in children's social care the Integrated Children's System
ushers in not only new ways of working but also new IT systems. Social work
practitioners will therefore require additional training to become confident in
using the system.

Prior to the implementation of the Integrated Children's System, approximately half the social work practitioners (52%) stated that they had received
training on one or more aspect of using IT. With the introduction of the Integrated Children's System training on IT increased significantly. Practically
three-quarters of staff (74%) reported receiving IT training following its
introduction in their authority.

The reports of practitioners suggest that the focus of IT training also
changed with the implementation of the Integrated Children's System (see
Table 4.2).

**Table 4.2 Practitioners' assessments
of amount of IT training received**

Task	Prior to implementation		Post implementation		Change
Use of the existing client index	11	46%	16	48%	2%
E-mail/inter/intranet	13	54%	5	15%	−39%
Use of the operating system	11	46%	3	9%	−37%
Word processing	8	33%	4	12%	−21%
Data entry	7	29%	21	64%	35%
Report generation	4	17%	4	12%	−5%
	n=24		n=33		

Less emphasis was placed on teaching 'core' computer skills such as e-mail, inter/intranet, word processing and use of the operating system, while data entry tasks were covered more thoroughly – features which changed as a result of the Integrated Children's System. This shift in emphasis reflects the changed focus of IT work undertaken by practitioners since implementation.

Sources of help

Previous research has shown that the delivery of one-off courses to introduce practitioners to new ways of working is not the most effective way to achieve and maintain a trained and confident staff group (Cleaver et al. 2004a). One-off training events cannot anticipate all the issues that can arise, the different knowledge bases or learning styles of staff, or the consequences of high staff turnover and staff shortages. For example, feedback from the pilot authorities suggests that at the start of their implementation programme staff were most frequently seeking help in relation to the new IT system; ensuring staff received IT training and support was essential. However, as the glitches were ironed out and practitioners became familiar with new forms of data entry they sought help over new ways of working.

To address these issues the participating local authorities put in place a range of means by which their social work practitioners could obtain help in relation to the Integrated Children's System. These included:

- telephone helplines
- experts or super-users
- administrative support
- additional IT training
- technical support.

Although all the sources of help covered assistance on practice changes, the primary focus was on enabling practitioners to use the authority's new IT system.

Despite the small numbers of respondents the findings suggest telephone helplines, technical support and experts or super-users were more quickly established by local authorities (see Table 4.3). It could be argued that other forms of support, such as additional training and administrative support, required greater resources and needed forward planning.

Table 4.3 Sources of help available to practitioners

Task	In place		Planned	
Telephone helpline	7	47%	1	7%
Experts/super-users	5	33%	4	29%
Admin support	3	20%	2	14%
Additional IT training	1	7%	7	50%
Technical support	6	40%	1	7%
	n=15		n=14	

At the time of the research, although practitioners valued the help they received to come to terms with new systems, it was too early to evaluate the effectiveness of the various methods of support.

Summary points

Fifty-two social work practitioners and managers provided information on their experience of the Integrated Children's System; a further 46 provided information on its impact on their use of IT.

Their responses suggest that insufficient training on the Integrated Children's System had hindered their understanding of the new ways of working with children and families.

Managers and practitioners reported that the Integrated Children's System had affected all aspects of recording practice with children and families. Perceived changes related to both the amount and quality of the information recorded.

Increases in recorded information reflected both positive outcomes of the new system, such as practice now conforming with Government Guidance and negative outcomes, such as inadequate software and IT systems.

Practitioners and managers' views on how the Integrated Children's System had impacted on the quality of recording were mixed. A similar proportion thought the quality had improved as thought it had deteriorated.

A number of practitioners and managers thought the Integrated Children's System formats were not family friendly and were having a negative impact on the quality of practice. Their comments suggest a confusion over the purpose of the formats, insufficient training and IT systems that, at the time of the study, were unable to produce family friendly 'outputs'.

Practitioners reported that the implementation of the Integrated Children's System had resulted in them spending more time at their computers. Some saw this as impacting negatively on their capacity to work with children and families. Their comments suggest that the increase in time spent inputting data was frequently the result of unresolved problems with IT systems.

Three-quarters of respondents reported receiving training on the new IT system. The focus of IT training changed with greater emphasis being placed on data entry tasks, reflecting the changing role IT played in social work practice. Managers and practitioners valued additional help from sources such as telephone helplines, super-users and administrative staff.

Chapter 5

Impact of the Integrated Children's System on Inter-Agency Working

Introduction

One of the key principles underpinning the Integrated Children's System is that of taking an inter-agency approach to working with children and families. When considering the impact of the Integrated Children's System, it must be acknowledged that its implementation has taken a significant amount of time during which other change initiatives which influence inter-agency working have been taking place (see Chapter 1). These include:

- The Children Act 2004
- Every Child Matters agenda
- Children and Young People: Rights to Action agenda
- Children's Trusts
- Framework Partnerships
- extended schools
- Strategy for Looked After Children
- Local Safeguarding Children Boards
- Information Sharing and Assessment
- e-government agenda
- Youth Justice and Respect agendas.

These initiatives also affected practitioners' working practices and throughout this chapter it is important to set the impact of the Integrated Children's
System within this wider context.

To understand the impact of the Integrated Children's System on collaborative working, information was gathered both before and after its implementation. A variety of methods were used including interviews, questionnaires,
focus groups and a scrutiny of recording formats routinely used by agencies
working with children, other than children's social care (see Appendix 1).
This chapter focuses on the context of inter-agency collaboration prior to
implementation of the Integrated Children's System before examining how it
impacts on inter-agency practice.

Inter-agency collaboration prior to implementation

A key objective of gathering data prior to the implementation of the Integrated Children's System was to understand current practice with regard to
inter-agency collaboration and information sharing. To achieve this information was gathered through:

- an examination of blank copies of the formats used to record
  information about children and families; social services recording
  formats were not included as these had been the subject of careful
  scrutiny through the audit of children's social care case files (see
  Chapter 3)

- interviews with practitioners and managers across five agencies
  (children's social care, health, education, youth offending teams and
  the police)

- a questionnaire based on the interview schedule sent to all
  professionals working with children and families within the five
  agencies.

The content of recording formats (excluding those from children's social care)

All agencies must record information about the children and families they
work with. The scrutiny of 169 recording formats, submitted by health (92),
education (59), youth offending (13) and the police (5), showed that most
record personal data to identify the child as well as some additional information about the child's needs.

PERSONAL INFORMATION ABOUT A CHILD

The Data Protection Act 1998 defines personal data as 'data which relate to a living individual who can be identified (a) from those data...' (Data Protection Act 1998, Part 1, 1 (1)). To ensure no misunderstandings or mistakes of identity occur when information is to be shared to support collaborative working, it is essential that this accurately identifies the child. The Common Assessment Framework, for example, requires professionals to record the child's name, address, date of birth and gender in terms of male or female (HM Government 2006b).

How personal information is recorded will affect the ease with which data can be exchanged. Although minor differences, such as recording the child's gender using the different categories (such as male/female or girl/boy), can be accommodated when information is exchanged manually, this will not be possible when electronic transfer of data is introduced.

Finally, it is essential for professionals from different disciplines and working situations to have a common understanding of the language used to describe children's needs and circumstances. For example, although all practitioners will interpret terms such as gender or date of birth in the same way, other expressions such as the child's home address is open to interpretation. For example, for a looked after child this could refer to the address of the child's birth parents or current foster or residential home. Moreover, the professional discipline, training and experience will affect practitioners' understanding. For example, expressions such as health surveillance or developmental checks have specific meaning to those with a medical background but may be less clearly understood by those from other disciplines.

In most cases the formats used by health, education, youth offending teams and the police recorded personal information about the child. However, as the following points show, the language used to record this showed considerable variation.

- Name of the child. Practically every one of the 169 formats (95.3%) asked for the full name of the child. However, this took 20 different forms, including: pupil's name, patient's name, forename, your name, young person's name, child's name, name of young person.

- Child's age. Similarly most formats (82.2%) recorded the child's age but five different terms were used.

- Child's address. Two-thirds of formats (65.7%) recorded where the child lived, but once again there was much variation. Ten different terms were identified, including: family address, contact address, child's address, address of family, patient's address, child's home address.

- Child's gender. Just over a quarter of formats (27.2%) recorded the child's gender. Six different terms were used, including: Male, Female, Male/Female, M/F, Boy/Girl.

- Child's family. Half the formats (50.3%) recorded details about the child's family. Once again how this was recorded showed considerable variation. The study identified 35 different ways this information was recorded, including: name of parents/carers, brief genogram, care arrangements, name of parents/guardians, family composition, about you, details of those living in the household.

OTHER KEY INFORMATION RELATING TO A CHILD

Information relating to the child's developmental needs, parenting capacity and family and environmental factors was also recorded on many formats, although this differed both in what was asked for and the terminology used.

- Child's health. Well over half of the 169 formats (60.4%) recorded general information about a child's health, 17 enabled the child's immunisations to be noted, and 9 the results of 'developmental checks'. However, there was little consistency in how these terms were to be interpreted. For example, immunisations could relate to all immunisations or to immunisations relevant to the child's age. Developmental checks included: developmental checks relating to the child's current age, health surveillance, developmental history, developmental assessments.

- Child's education. A similar proportion of formats (54.4%) recorded information about the child's school, although 24 different expressions were used. In addition, 70 formats recorded information about the child's educational progress, although how this was to be judged varied considerably. For example, 27 formats recorded general information about the child's educational achievements; 5 recorded SATs; 3 recorded GCSEs; 21 SENs using ten different terms. Twenty-six formats asked about school attendance, while 11 asked about school absence, and 10 about school exclusion.

- Other aspects of children's development. The formats were less likely to enable information about other aspects of children's development to be recorded. For example, the child's emotional and behavioural development was recorded on 49 formats (29%), family and social relationships on 33 (19.5%), and 14 different ways of asking for this information were identified, including: socialisation, relevant family information, how the young person relates to adults and peers. The child's identity was recorded on 7 formats; the child's social presentation on 6; self-care skills on 10; and 15 formats asked about offending behaviour (nine different ways of asking for this information were identified, including: offence details and criminal history, harm-related behaviour, offence details, what you think about crime and your future). Finally, 4 formats recorded parenting skills and 14 formats recorded information about the wider family and environment.

Professionals' views on collaborative working prior to the Integrated Children's System

To gain a comprehensive understanding of collaborative working prior to the implementation of the Integrated Children's System it was essential that the views of a diverse group of professionals working with children informed the study. Interviews and questionnaires were therefore targeted at the statutory agencies working with children.

A total of 131 professionals were either interviewed or returned completed questionnaires: 52 from within children's social care, 19 from health, 32 from education, 3 from the police and 25 from YOTs. The group were fairly equally split between managers (accounting for 59%) and practitioners (accounting for 41%).

The confidence with which professionals exchange information and work collaboratively may be affected by their qualifications and experience (Cleaver *et al.* 2004b). Eighty-eight per cent of respondents had a professional qualification with 65 per cent qualified for ten years or more. Fifty-one per cent (n=130) had worked for over five years in the agency.

THE CHILDREN THEY WORK WITH

Collaborative working and information sharing is key to safeguarding and promoting the welfare of children. However, the processes differ depending not only on the identity of the agency but also on the group of children with whom they work. For example, in child protection work and work with children looked after there are well-defined procedures for sharing information, but when working with children in need who are living at home, the process is less clear. It was essential, therefore, that professionals working with children in a variety of different circumstances were included in the sample. Over half the group (56%) reported that they routinely worked with vulnerable children (those at risk of social exclusion or in need of protection), 56 per cent worked regularly with children looked after, 12 per cent with children in adoption proceedings, and almost two-fifths with children involved in offending.

IN WHAT CIRCUMSTANCES WAS INFORMATION SHARED?

> Good information sharing is the key to successful collaborative working and early intervention to help children and young people at risk of poor outcomes. (www.everychildmatters.gov.uk)

The factors that support good information sharing and inter-agency collaboration to safeguard and promote the welfare of children have been identified by much previous research (see, for example, Birchall and Hallett 1995; Cleaver *et al.* 2007; Kroll and Taylor 2003). This body of research suggests that the key factors are:

- understanding and respecting the roles and responsibilities of other services
- good communication
- regular contact and meetings
- common priorities
- inter-agency training
- clear guidelines and procedures for working together.

The current study reinforces these findings. Practically every practitioner (98%) reported that personal contacts and professional networks guided their work with other agencies. They identified a number of ways which enabled such personal contacts to develop including inter-agency training, regular meetings, joint working arrangements and multi-agency forums.

Practitioners reported that personal contacts enabled them to easily clarify or resolve issues. For example, one health professional's observation illustrates the extent to which personal contacts were valued:

> Enormously – it is essential to have personal contact within other agencies to be able to understand each other's point of view, to ask more easily for advice and for clarification of issues of concern.

Personal contacts were also used to resolve confusion and uncertainty over the impact of data protection legislation on what information can be shared and in what circumstances. However, practitioners were clear that professional contacts on their own were not enough and needed to be set within a formal framework of clear policies and procedures. Where policies and procedures were not in place information sharing relied on personal contacts, a situation which could result in inconsistencies in practice and a failure to work within the law and government legislation and guidance.

Information sharing and collaborative working to safeguard and promote the welfare of children varied depending on the issue under discussion. Practitioners reported that information sharing was most effective when there were safeguarding concerns about a child, when a child was disabled, or where there were concerns over a child's health or education. Information sharing was viewed as adequate when there were concerns over the effects on a child of social exclusion, poverty and housing. In contrast, when concerns related to the parents, such as parental mental health, drug and alcohol abuse, learning disabilities or domestic violence, information sharing was seen as least effective. Practitioners cited a number of reasons for the reluctance to share information in these circumstances, including: infrequent contact between children and adult services meant informal relationships which support information sharing were not developed; adult services were seen as not being child focused; and protocols for information sharing between children and adult services had not always been agreed. This is of particular concern given the wealth of information demonstrating the link between these issues and childhood vulnerability (Cleaver *et al.* 1999).

SUPPORTS AND BARRIERS TO EFFECTIVE COLLABORATION

Practitioners identified factors that supported effective collaboration and those that hampered it.

Factors supporting effective collaboration included:

- joint commitment and focus
- good and regular communication and, if possible, continuity of personal contacts (joint training was often cited as a forum for developing contacts)
- effective policies, procedures and structures
- good understanding of the roles and responsibilities of professionals across all agencies; this can allow a common focus and sense of purpose to develop
- discussions and meetings in order to break down barriers
- protocols for information sharing.

The barriers identified by practitioners were often the obverse of the issues identified as supporting effective inter-agency working and included:

- A lack of communication between agencies, in particular:
    ◦ Difficulties in making the initial contact. Different working structures could become a barrier, for example school timetables made contacting teachers difficult, and highly structured working practices could hamper contact with GPs.

    ◦ A lack of feedback. Practitioners were concerned about sharing information when there was little or no feedback about what happened to the information they had provided or the outcome for the child and family. The difficulties were particularly acute in relation to hearing the results of referrals and assessments carried out by children's social care.

    ◦ Lack of policies, procedures, guidance and clear structures for sharing information.

    ◦ Lack of engagement from agencies due to different priorities. This was most keenly felt when relevant practitioners failed to attend key meetings.

- Different priorities and working cultures between adult and children's services. Practitioners reported that some services working with adults were not always willing to share information about their clients. For example, practitioners in children's services reported difficulties in obtaining information about how parental mental illness or substance misuse might affect the safety and welfare of children they were working with. These findings reinforce those from previous research which identified that, when children are not the primary focus of an agency's work, concerns over the safety and welfare of the children are not always the priority (Cleaver et al. 2007; Murphy and Oulds 2000). The Children Act 2004, the National Service Framework for Children, Young People and Maternity Services (Department of Health and Department for Education and Skills 2004) and Working Together to Safeguard Children (HM Government 2006c) have helped to raise awareness that the safeguarding and welfare of children is everyone's responsibility. This should resolve perceived inconsistencies between different legislative frameworks.

- Different thresholds for services between agencies in relation to what constitutes a vulnerable child or a child in need. The introduction of the Common Assessment Framework will establish a common language to describe children's needs, ensure more specific referrals and should result in greater clarity over the thresholds for services. In addition, a function of the Local Safeguarding Children Board is to establish 'the action to be taken where there are concerns about a child's safety or welfare, including thresholds for intervention' (HM Government 2006c, p.78, 3.18 (a) (i)).

- Inadequate understanding of the roles, responsibilities and services other agencies provide.

- Lack of resources within all agencies both in terms of staff and service provision.

- Parents not giving their agreement to the sharing of information.

Impact of the Integrated Children's System on inter-agency collaboration

At the point when the research team returned to the local authorities to assess the impact of the Integrated Children's System on inter-agency collaboration, as discussed earlier, one authority had not been able to complete their implementation and consequently only three authorities took part in this aspect of the study (see Appendix 1 for details).

Information was gathered from practitioners and managers who attended workshops where they were asked to complete a questionnaire on their experiences of the System. Seventy-eight attendees completed a questionnaire: 52 from within children's social care, 14 from health, 9 from education, 2 from the police and 1 from housing. The group were fairly equally split between managers (accounting for 47.4%) and practitioners (accounting for 52.6%). Their responses were used to examine how practitioners were prepared and trained for the Integrated Children's System and how it affected their day-to-day work in relation to:

- information requested from agencies
- assessments and reports completed by agencies
- information received by agencies
- electronic information exchange
- inter-agency practice.

Informing and training practitioners on the Integrated Children's System

All professionals who work with children and families will need to understand what the Integrated Children's System is and how it will impact on their practice. The findings suggest that some information on the Integrated Children's System was beginning to be provided to professionals working in all key agencies (see Chapter 2). For example, approximately half the respondents (52%) reported having attended a multi-agency briefing session. This group included representatives from all the agencies questioned (children's social care, education, health, police and housing).

Although most of the in-service training on the Integrated Children's System was delivered to practitioners in children's social care (see Chapter 4), nonetheless practically a quarter (23%) of practitioners in other agencies attended training provided by their own agency and three attended inter-agency training, suggesting such initiatives were still in their infancy at the time of the study.

The lack of sufficient training was keenly felt by practitioners who were often unclear about the relevance of the Integrated Children's System for their work with children and families.

> Had half day briefing about a year ago, but nothing since. (Shire County, Health professional)

The provision of multi-agency briefings and training was related to the extent to which local authorities had progressed in their implementation programme. Those such as the Welsh Local Authority which had managed to get systems running well (see Chapter 2) had been able to provide much more information and training. Three-quarters of respondents (76.5%) in the Welsh Local Authority had attended multi-agency briefing sessions on the Integrated Children's System, a rate twice that found in either of the other two authorities.

Impact on collaboration – changes to information requested from agencies

The findings suggest that the Integrated Children's System is making an impact on the information agencies are requesting from each other. Sixty-seven of the 78 professionals who attended the workshops provided information on the impact of the Integrated Children's System on the information they were being asked for. Just under half the group (43.3%) reported receiving requests from other agencies for different information as a result of implementation, information which would help build a more holistic picture of the child's needs.

Practitioners and managers in children's social care reported that a range of agencies were seeking different information. Although education and health were those most frequently responsible for requests for different information, other agencies are also beginning to be affected. A few social workers reported that requests for information from the following services had changed as a result of the Integrated Children's System: police, probation, housing, youth offending teams and housing.

Practitioners from agencies other than children's social care (in most cases this was education and health) also reported that the Integrated Children's System had affected the information that was requested from them. A similar pattern of change was reported; the agencies most frequently seeking different information were children's social care, education and health, with the police, youth offending teams and the Connexions services being noted on a few occasions.

The closer integration of children's social care, health and education reflects the emphasis within the participating authorities to improve collaborative working. For example, the Welsh Local Authority developed an electronic exchange of information between schools and children's social services; nominated members of staff within the schools had access to restricted information on children held on the Integrated Children's System database in children's social services. The Shire County had developed protocols for sharing information about the health of looked after children between health and children's social care. All the authorities were working towards greater collaboration with the police and probation service.

CHANGES TO THE QUANTITY AND QUALITY OF INFORMATION REQUESTED

In the majority of cases where requests for information had been affected, changes related to the type of information other agencies requested rather than any increase in the amount or quality of the information sought. For example, over half (56%) of those who thought requests had changed reported no changes in the amount or quality of information that was sought. When changes were reported they were generally in a positive direction; practically a third of respondents (31%) were asked for more information, and a similar proportion (27.6%) for better quality information. The findings show that most of those who thought they were being asked for more information also thought that the quality of the information requested had improved (see Table 5.1).

Table 5.1 Changes to the amount and quality of information requested from practitioners

	Change in quantity		Change in quality	
Reduced	6.9%	N=2	10.3%	N=3
No change	48.3%	N=14	44.8%	N=13
Increased	31.0%	N=9	27.6%	N=8
No answer	13.8%	N=4	17.2%	N=5
n=29				

Impact on collaboration – changes to assessments and reports completed by agencies other than children's social care

Although the Integrated Children's System impacts profoundly on the work of social work practitioners (as discussed in Chapter 4) professionals in other agencies and organisations will be affected when their work involves children receiving services from children's social care.

The findings suggest that the influence of the Integrated Children's System on the way information is recorded by services for children, other than social care, was small but, nonetheless, encouraging. For example, a teacher in the Shire County noted that reports for children's social care now included educational attainment, Special Educational Needs (SEN) information, school exclusions and contributions to Personal Education Plans (PEPs). Similarly, a health worker in the Shire County noted that the Integrated Children's System had affected the way she wrote Child Protection Conference and Core Group reports.

Impact on collaboration – changes to information received by agencies

Approximately three-quarters of participants (57 of 78) provided information on the impact of the Integrated Children's System on the assessments and reports they received. The findings suggest that two-thirds (n=37) thought that the reports and assessments sent to them had changed.

Over three-quarters (77.5%) of the 52 respondents working in children's social care reported that the assessments and records they received had changed as a result of the Integrated Children's System. In most cases, the changes related to records and assessments completed within their own agency. However, changes were also beginning to be experienced in the paperwork received from other agencies. The following example illustrates changes in the assessments carried out by housing and it is of interest to note that agencies other than social services were starting to bring their practice closer in line with the Integrated Children's System.

> Housing providers' assessments and reviews are starting to reflect the dimensions within the Pathway Plan. (Welsh Local Authority, practitioner)

Responses from health and education professionals show that, as would be expected, they were receiving newly formatted assessments and reports as a result of the implementation of the Integrated Children's System. The paperwork most frequently referred to were reviews on looked after children and Child Protection Conference reports. For example, an educationalist in the Shire County noted changes in the Chair's reports from the LAC reviews they received, and a health worker experienced changes to LAC reviews, and Child Protection Conference reports.

The perceptions of health professionals were mixed; some found the new formats too long whereas others appreciated the improvements to the quality of information.

> Reports received contain more information. (Shire County, Health)

> Very wordy and repetitive. All repeated information for each child and family history/support. (Shire County, Health)

> Core Group update is more in-depth. (Shire County, Health)

Impact on collaboration – changes to information exchanged electronically

Forty-three practitioners commented on the impact of the Integrated Children's System on information exchanged electronically. Their responses suggest the electronic exchange of information had not been greatly affected by the system at the time of the study.

> Other agencies in the area are not using ICS, therefore information exchange is still by the same means as prior to implementation. (Welsh Local Authority, Children's social services)

Two-thirds of practitioners (67.4%) experienced no change in the extent of electronic information exchange, a not unexpected finding because at the time of the research no authority's IT system allowed direct two-way transfer of data between different agencies. Authorities were focusing most of their energies on embedding the system within children's social care. Nonetheless, initiatives were being developed in two of the authorities to enable greater collaborative working through enabling other agencies limited access to the children's social care data-base (see Chapter 7 for further details).

> The authority is currently looking at how this can be developed/enhanced to export and import records electronically. (Shire County, Children's social care)

> PEPs are now electronic and target section is in the ICS format. (Welsh Local Authority, Education)

The findings, however, do suggest that things are beginning to change in that 13 practitioners (30.2%) reported an increase in the amount of information that was now being electronically exchanged. Most of those who had experienced an increase worked in the Welsh Local Authority. Their reports suggest the increase in sending information electronically was not confined to a particular agency and they identified the following organisations as those with whom electronically transferred information had increased: children's social care, education (head teachers, designated teachers, teachers, special education needs workers), educational welfare officers, health (health visitors, community nurses, paediatricians), youth offending teams, Children and Family Court Advisory and Support Service (CAFCASS), Child and Adolescent Mental Health Services (CAMHS), and social workers based in other local authorities. Finally, one practitioner reported a decrease in the electronic transfer of information.

Impact on collaboration – changes to inter-agency practice

Practitioners were asked to assess the impact of the Integrated Children's System on inter-agency working with regard to the following agencies: children's social care, education, health, police and youth offending teams. Their views were sought on four areas of inter-agency work:

- policy and practice
- information sharing
- clarification of roles and responsibilities
- quality of inter-agency working.

By definition practitioners were not commenting about their own agency; for example, the 52 professionals from children's social care provided information on the impact of the Integrated Children's System on some aspects of inter-agency issues in relation to the police, youth offending, health and education. Consequently, because the greatest number of respondents were based in children's social care, the smallest number of responses were available with regard to this service.

Regardless of the area of inter-agency work under consideration, most professionals (more than 68 per cent in each case) who responded assessed the position as not having changed as a result of the Integrated Children's System. When change was reported, in the majority of cases professionals were optimistic in their reports as the following detailed breakdown illustrates.

CHILDREN'S SOCIAL CARE

Over half of professionals (8 of 14) from agencies other than children's social care thought the Integrated Children's System had not affected any aspect of their agency's working practice with this organisation. Where changes were identified, three health professionals and one teacher thought that things had improved.

> SSD now have the IT reports, add other agencies' reports to theirs – not always in original words. (Shire County, Health)

In contrast, one educationalist reported it had resulted in more confusion over roles and responsibilities, and one health professional considered it had negatively affected the quality of inter-agency working.

HEALTH SERVICE

Two-thirds of professionals (31 of 45) thought that the Integrated Children's System had not impacted on any aspect of their agency's work with the health service. In contrast 12 reported a positive impact on all or some areas of work with the health service, and 2 (1 teacher and 1 social worker) some negative effects.

> Looked After Children health visitor has viewing access to ICS. Looking to pilot access to ICS for generic health visitors and installing ICS in GP surgeries. Expanding electronic Child Protection register. (Welsh Local Authority, Children's social services)

> A health visitor attached to duty and this has led to greater awareness of the different roles using ICS. (London Borough, Children's social care)

EDUCATION SERVICE

The findings for education are very similar to that found for the health service. Two-thirds of respondents (31 of 45) reported no changes in any aspect of their agency's work with the education service. In many cases this reflected practitioners' awareness of the Integrated Children's System. For example, a health worker in the Shire County noted 'Not aware of ICS, how it works and who it is for', therefore not using anything different when discussing possible changes to inter-agency working with the education service.

In all cases those who reported a change were optimistic in their perceptions.

> Pilot of electronic information exchange with schools has developed as a consequence of ICS. (Welsh Local Authority, Children's social services)

> The introduction of PEPs and LAC coordinator has assisted this process. (Welsh Local Authority, Children's social services)

> The SEN department is still very fixed in their approach with working together. The introduction of the Tripartite Panel for funding has helped. (London Borough, Children's social care)

Although approximately a third of professionals thought that the Integrated Children's System had positively affected their agency's work with the education service and the health service, a much smaller proportion thought it had impacted on work with the police service or youth offending teams.

POLICE SERVICE

The police and children's social care have developed policies and procedures and close working relationships to ensure children are safeguarded. This emphasis on collaborative working is reinforced in the revised government guidance on Working Together to Safeguard Children (HM Government 2006c).

> The police hold important information about children who may be at risk of harm as well as those who cause such harm. They are committed to sharing information and intelligence with other organisations where this is necessary to protect children. (HM Government 2006c, p.61, paragraph 2.101)

However, this emphasis on greater collaboration does not appear to have been greatly promoted by the implementation of the Integrated Children's System. Over three-quarters (40/51) of respondents thought collaboration with the police was problematic and the implementation of the Integrated Children's System had failed to promote better working relations.

> Police involvement remains low as it did with the Framework for Assessment. (Shire County, Children's social care)

> Do the police tell you anything? (London Borough, Children's social care)

Nonetheless, when change was acknowledged this was generally positive; 8 professionals reported an improvement with regard to working relations with the police, although 3 thought they had worsened.

> Police have been extremely proactive in progressing the ICS. (Welsh Local Authority, Children's social services)

> We receive information far more quickly. (Welsh Local Authority, Children's social services)

YOUTH OFFENDING TEAMS

The revised government guidance also stresses the importance of youth offending teams working collaboratively with children's services.

> It is necessary, therefore, for there to be clear links between youth justice and LA children's social care, both at a strategic level and at a child-specific operational level. (HM Government 2006c, p.65, paragraph 2.116)

Most respondents (40/46) reported that the Integrated Children's System had not impacted on inter-agency practice with youth offending teams (YOTs) in any of the four areas of work. Their comments provide insights into what impeded closer working relationships, and suggest a number of factors such as: the priority given to this work; the mismatch between different assessment frameworks; and unresolved difficulties over information sharing.

> YOT ICS sub-group about to be established – this has been left while activity has concentrated on health, education and police. (Welsh Local Authority, Children's social services)

> YOT have a very clear mandate in terms of their role and this causes problems in terms of the interface. Very little quality information sharing and very little achieved in terms of linking ASSET[1] with the Assessment Framework. (Welsh Local Authority, Children's social services)

> Problems for YOT completing some of ICS forms on remand. (Shire County, Children's social care)

The findings indicate that, when the Integrated Children's System was thought to have affected inter-agency working, the changes were generally seen as positive. The opinions of practitioners varied across the three participating authorities and it is clear that some pilots had advanced further in this work than others. For example, the majority of practitioners who identified

---

1   A structured assessment tool used by youth offending teams.

improvements in inter-agency working came from the Welsh Local Authority and the Shire County.

These authorities had established initiatives to improve collaborative relations between children's social care and other children's services, one with education and the other with health. For example, the Welsh Local Authority had taken a proactive approach and used the Integrated Children's System to promote information sharing. It had established specific inter-agency work groups with education and health to explore how the system could support their workers. This resulted in the development of pilots enabling head teachers read-only access to parts of its Integrated Children's System, an initiative which was subsequently extended to health, with police and probation also expressing an interest in developing pilots. This approach involved considerable commitment from and work by staff in children's social services. However, it was successful in getting the active engagement of partner agencies who were able to see real and tangible benefits of being involved in the Integrated Children's System. The authority was able to build on the goodwill created, as word spread between agencies about the benefits of the Integrated Children's System, with some agencies requesting more active involvement.

Summary points

A scrutiny of blank formats used by health, education, youth offending teams and the police showed that the language used to record information about children and families varied considerably. Although variations can be accommodated when information is exchanged manually, a common language will be needed to allow electronic transfer.

The views of 131 professionals (from children's social care, health, education, youth offending teams and the police) provided insights into collaborative working and information sharing prior to the introduction of the Integrated Children's System. Their responses suggest personal contacts and professional networks guided their work with other agencies. Practitioners emphasised the need for clear information-sharing policies and procedures.

Only three local authorities had implemented the Integrated Children's System at the point of follow-up. Seventy-eight professionals, from a range of agencies, provided information on the impact of the Integrated Children's System on inter-agency collaboration.

Approximately half the respondents reported attending a multi-agency briefing session that explained the Integrated Children's System. The availability of briefing sessions for workers outside of children's social care depended on how advanced local authorities were in their implementation programme.

The Integrated Children's System affected the type of information agencies requested from one another. The exchange of information between children's social care, health and education was most affected. Practitioners reported that as a result of the Integrated Children's System professionals from these agencies were requesting more and better quality information.

The findings suggest that the Integrated Children's System is beginning to impact on the way agencies other than children's social care record information about the children they work with.

The Integrated Children's System has affected the reports and assessments received by agencies working with children. In most cases social workers were experiencing changes in the reports and assessments from colleagues within their own organisation. Professionals in health and education reported changes to the documentation they received from children's social care. The changes had a mixed reception; practitioners welcomed the increased focus and quality of information but resented any duplication.

The Integrated Children's System has started to impact on the amount of information exchanged electronically between agencies working with children. As initiatives to improve collaborative practice develop this is likely to increase. The pilot authorities were at different stages of introducing electronic data exchange.

The majority of professionals thought that the introduction of the Integrated Children's System had not affected inter-agency work. However, when changes were reported, in the majority of cases professionals saw these as improvements in inter-agency collaboration.

The increase in inter-agency collaboration was greatest between health, education and children's social care and to a lesser degree between these agencies and the police and youth offending teams. The findings suggest improved inter-agency collaboration was dependent on the existing culture of inter-agency working, the approach to implementing the Integrated Children's System and the stage of development.

Chapter 6

Impact of the Integrated Children's System on Involving Children and Young People

Introduction

The Children Act 1989 anticipated the United Nations Convention on the Rights of the Child (1989) and together they have established the rights of children to participate in decision making that affects their lives.

The Children Act 1989 and the accompanying Guidance and Regulations place a duty on local authorities:

- to ascertain the wishes and feelings of children and young people (having regard to their age and understanding) and take these into account before any Care Plans or court decision are made
- to invite them to attend and participate actively in reviews and other planning meetings
- to notify them of the decisions that have been reached at planning and review meetings
- to inform them of what services and resources are available. (Department of Health 1991)

The Children Act 2004 amends sections 17, 20 and 47 of the Children Act 1989 so that, so far as is reasonable, children's wishes and feelings are ascertained and taken into consideration regarding the provision of services or actions to be taken that affect them.

The Convention on the Rights of the Child (1989), accepted by the UK Government since 1991, is entirely congruent with these principles. It includes three main sets of rights for children: the right to protection from abuse and exploitation; the right to provision of services; and the right to participation in decision making. Of particular relevance for the focus of this chapter is Article 12.1.

> Parties shall assure to the child who is capable of forming his or her own views the right to express those views freely in all matters affecting the child, the views of the child being given due weight in accordance with the age and maturity of the child.

The importance of consulting children and young people is underpinned by the Departments of Health's Quality Protects programme (Department of Health 1989) and the National Service Framework for Children, Young People and Maternity Services (Department of Health and Department for Education and Skills 2004). The National Service Framework sets national standards for children's health and social care which require services to 'give children, young people and their parents increased information, power and choice over the support and treatment they receive, and involve them in planning their care and services' (Department of Health and Department for Education and Skills 2004, p.9).

The Government Guidance on the Children Act 1989 provided the basis for developing the Looking After Children materials, designed to support assessment, planning and review for looked after children, and implemented in almost all local authorities by 1999 (see Scott 1999). Additional Guidance was issued under section 7 of the Local Authority Social Services Act 1970 to support assessments of children in need and their families, along with practice guidance and specific resources (Department for Education and Skills 2006b; Department of Health 2000; Department of Health et al. 2000b). Recent Government Guidance to support the Children Act 2004 continues to underpin the importance of ascertaining children's wishes and feelings (HM Government 2005c, 2006b).

Consistent throughout all the Guidance is the emphasis on seeking and recording the views of children on all processes that affect them. For example, the Integrated Children's System states that planning should wherever possible be a process which fully involves the child or young person and children and young people should participate as fully as possible in the review process (Department of Health 2002b).

However, introducing new legislation and guidance and developing supportive materials does not always bring about the expected changes to practice. For example, research that explores social work practice since the implementation of the Children Act 1989 suggests there has been some improvement to the extent to which children and young people are involved in decision making, although there is much still to be accomplished. For example, research by Grimshaw and Sinclair (1997) indicates that the regulatory framework introduced by the Children Act 1989 did increase the participation of children and young people in reviews. However, although most young people were consulted about their wishes and feelings and reported that they had attended reviews, they did not necessarily feel that they had participated successfully. Moreover, they had received little information to help them understand the planning process or support and help them through it. Review meetings were experienced as formal meetings where young people found it difficult to express their views and feelings, particularly when strangers were present; no child or young person interviewed about reviews enjoyed them.

This chapter explores the extent to which the implementation of the Integrated Children's System (which supports the Children Act 1989) has impacted on social work practice with regard to the involvement of children and young people in decision making that affects them. The first part establishes the wider context within which the views and experiences of young people can be set while the second focuses on looked after children and explores their experiences and involvement in planning and reviews since the introduction of the Integrated Children's System. Limited time and resources meant that it was not possible to include all children and young people in contact with children's social care. Because there is some information, albeit very limited, on the impact of the Assessment Framework on the involvement of children in need in assessments and decisions that affect them (Cleaver *et al.* 2004b), the focus of this study has been on young people looked after.

Information is drawn from two primary sources: the two-stage scrutiny of social work case records and postal questionnaires completed by young people looked after (see Appendix 1).

The involvement of children and young people: findings from the scrutiny of social work records

A variety of data has been used to explore the impact of the Integrated Children's System on consulting and involving children and young people in assessments, planning and review, including findings from previous research and the two-stage scrutiny of social work records (see Appendix 1 for details). However, the information social workers were required to record altered with the introduction of the Integrated Children's System. For example, prior to implementation social workers were not expected to record whether they had discussed the findings from the initial assessment with the child or young person, a requirement of the Integrated Children's System. In some instances, therefore, no base-line is available from which to measure change. A further issue to impact on the ability to assess change was the lack of detailed recording. For example, earlier research found that social workers recorded whether a copy of the initial assessment had been given to the family in 60 per cent of cases; no information was available in the remaining cases (Cleaver *et al.* 2004b). The findings from this study suggest the situation has remained remarkably constant; this information was found on the Integrated Children's System in 59 per cent of cases.

Assessments

INITIAL ASSESSMENTS

One way of ensuring that children and their families are informed of the decisions that have been made as a result of the initial assessment is to provide them with a copy of the assessment record. Previous research suggests that although approximately a third of parents are given copies of the assessment record it is rare for young people to be provided with copies (Cleaver *et al.* 2004b). Prior to the Integrated Children's System social workers were not expected to record particularly whether young people had been informed of the findings from the assessment.

Providing copies of official documentation may not be the most appropriate way of passing on information to children and young people. Most children appreciate social workers who explain what is going on during the assessment and provide them with some record of the decisions that had been made.

I wanted more explanation of what was happening. She [the social worker] said she would ring but she didn't. I did not really know what was happening and why. (16-year-old quoted in Cleaver *et al.* 2004b, p.93)

Young people want their social worker to talk them through the decisions which have been taken as a result of the assessment. Prior to the Integrated Children's System whether such a discussion had taken place was not routinely noted on case records; it is now a requirement to record this information. However, changes to records do not always result in the information being recorded. The scrutiny of 82 initial assessments post implementation found that whether social workers had discussed the assessment report with the child or young person was noted in 47 cases (57.3%). These data show that in only 6 of these cases (12.7%) had the social worker discussed the report with the child or young person. In 27 cases (57.4%) the social worker had indicated that discussing the report was inappropriate due to the child's age or understanding, and in a further 14 cases (29.7%) the record showed that no discussion had taken place. A scrutiny of the 41 cases, where the report had not been discussed with the child, reveals that the majority of the children were either very young (17 children were under the age of three years) or had a learning or communication disability (n=11). However, in practically a third of cases (n=13, 31.7%) there were no apparent barriers noted on the Integrated Children's System to discussing the report with the child or young person.

An exploration of the factors that social workers should consider in gauging children's capacity to understand can be found in Reder and Duncan (2003). Morris (1998) has argued that disabled children are often unnecessarily excluded from consultation, and Connors and Stalker (2005) have demonstrated how disabled children aged seven and over can be readily included in consultation.

Meetings
CHILD PROTECTION CONFERENCES
When enquiries under s47 of the Children Act 1989 have substantiated concerns about a child, managers in children's social care should ensure that a child protection conference is convened for the purpose of assessing all the relevant information and plan how to safeguard the child and promote his or her welfare. Government Guidance is clear that children should be appropriately involved.

> This includes talking to them about the purpose of the conference, the means by which they want to express their wishes and feelings (including by attending), as well as what they want said to whom and sharing the conference reports with them in advance. (HM Government 2006d, p.33, paragraph 45.1)

Child protection conferences were held for 44 children in the audit undertaken prior to the implementation of the Integrated Children's System: 22 children under the age of 5 years and 22 aged 5 years or more. After implementation child protection conferences involved 43 children: 18 under the age of 5 years and 25 aged 5 years or more. Although it could be argued that children younger than 5 years may not be able to express their views, there is considerable work that suggests even very young children and those with complex needs can be involved in decisions that concern them (see, for example, Jones 2003; Marchant 2001).

The scrutiny of social workers' records prior to implementation suggests children and young people were rarely involved; their views were generally not sought, the report was rarely discussed with them, and few were provided with a copy. In only 2 of 44 cases were young people's comments noted and the report discussed with them, and only one young person was provided with a copy. In 27 cases social workers reasoned that children were too young.

The study of the 43 records of child protection conferences since the implementation suggests little has changed. The comments of children and young people were found to have been recorded in only 6 cases (13.9%); in 4 of these cases social workers had also discussed the report with the child.

A scrutiny of the reasons for this low level of involvement reveals that, in 16 of the 37 cases where children or young people's comments had not been recorded, social workers had noted that it had not been appropriate to involve children because of their age or the complexity of their needs. An exploration of the remaining children reveals that three were under the age of 2 years and two had learning and behavioural disabilities. These leaves 16 children for whom age or disability should not have been a barrier to their involvement: six were aged between 5 and 9 years, nine aged between 10 and 14 years and one aged 15 years or more; none had learning or communication difficulties.

Plans

CHILD OR YOUNG PERSON'S PLAN

The child or young person's plan sets out the agency's plan for children living in the community, based on an analysis of the findings from a core assessment.

These plans were examined to discover the extent to which social workers consulted young people and recorded their views. Two pieces of recording on the Integrated Children's System were scrutinised: the section titled 'Child/young person's comments on the plan', and the section where children and young people are expected to sign the document to indicate that they have seen the plan. The data from 35 plans post implementation were compared with similar data collected from 30 plans prior to the implementation of the Integrated Children's System.

The findings from these sections suggest low levels of participation post implementation. In 18 cases social workers indicated that children's age or understanding prevented them from being involved. However, in only one of the remaining 17 cases had the social worker recorded the young person's comments and in no case was a young person's signature found on the document, although in two cases social workers had noted that the young person had refused to sign the document. This finding reflects practice before the Integrated Children's System. The scrutiny of the plans prior to implementation revealed the child or young person's signature in only three cases.

CARE PLANS

Both before and after the implementation of the Integrated Children's System social workers are expected to note whether the care plan has been discussed with the child and to record whether he or she agrees to it.

A record of the child's views was found in approximately half (52.4%) of the 63 care plans included in the scrutiny of social work records prior to implementation. Social work records post implementation suggest little has changed; a record of children's views about the plan was found in less than half (48.7%) of the 39 care plans scrutinised. Examining the remaining cases (n=20) shows this decision may have had some veracity; in ten cases social workers had recorded that it was inappropriate to discuss the plan with the child because of their age or understanding.

However, not recording the views for the remaining ten children was only reported in three instances. For seven children there was no apparent reason why their views had not been recorded; three were aged between 5 and 9 years, one aged between 10 and 14 years and three were 15 years or more.

PATHWAY PLANS

> The Children (Leaving Care) Act 2000 requires a Pathway Plan for all eligible, relevant and former relevant young people. The Pathway Plan fulfils the requirements both for assessing the young person's needs and planning services. It is divided into two parts. Part One records the assessed needs of the young person. Part Two sets out the services that are required to respond to the identified needs and to provide support during the transition to adulthood. The Pathway Plan replaces Part Two of the Care Plan and Assessment and Progress Record for all eligible children, and is informed by previous Care Plans, Reviews and Assessment and Progress Records. (Department of Health and Department for Education and Skills 2000–2005, Briefing Paper No.5, p.5)

It was routine practice to involve young people in both parts of their Pathway Plan. Government Regulations and Guidance (Department of Health 2001a) emphasises the importance of involving young people in Pathway Plans.

> Each young person will be central to drawing up their own plan, setting out their own goals and identifying with their personal adviser how the local authority will help them. The authority should work to ensure that the Plan is owned by the young person and is able to respond to their changing needs and ambitions. (Department of Health 2001a, p.40, paragraph 20)

A scrutiny of the 17 Pathway Plans post implementation shows that in all but one case the young person had been involved in the first part of the plan – the assessment. Information about their involvement in the second part of the plan had not been noted in two cases and in 12 cases (70.5%) young people had been involved. This rate of involvement is higher than was found prior to the implementation of the Integrated Children's System where the social work records showed just over half the young people (58.3%) were involved in their Pathway Plan. The findings suggest the Integrated Children's System may be having a positive impact on the involvement of young people in Pathway Plans.

Reviews

At the time of the study insufficient Child in Need reviews had been completed to allow any comments to be made.

CHILD PROTECTION REVIEWS

Thirty-two child protection reviews were included in the first audit of social work case files and 22 in audit post implementation. A scrutiny of the reviews, both prior and post the introduction of the Integrated Children's System, shows few children were consulted and attended child protection reviews. Prior to the Integrated Children's System only one child was consulted and attended their child protection review whereas post implementation, although social workers attempted to consult children in six cases, only three children wanted to be involved and attended their review.

Age and understanding was a barrier to involvement for a considerable proportion of children, accounting for the non-involvement of the child in 59 per cent of cases in the first audit and 33.3 per cent in the second. In the remaining cases information on whether children had been consulted had not been recorded.

LOOKED AFTER REVIEWS

The findings for reviews of looked after children reflect those found in relation to plans: children's involvement increased once they became looked after. This may reflect a longer tradition of consulting looked after children and including them in formal planning and reviewing processes. Consultation is supported by a wealth of documentation produced both nationally and locally to facilitate the implementation of the Looking After Children initiative (Scott 1999). The Integrated Children's System reiterates the messages from both Government Guidance and Looking After Children by making it clear that children and young people should be consulted prior to their review meetings about the date, time, venue, agenda and who should participate (Department of Health 1991, Vol 3).

Both the recording formats about reviews for looked after children used before and after implementation of the Integrated Children's System allowed social workers to record their consultation with young people and young people's attendance.

Seventy reviews of looked after children were scrutinised pre implementation. These show that social workers had recorded where children had been consulted in 53 cases (75.7%) and whether they attended their reviews in 64 cases (91.4%). A scrutiny of these data shows 81 per cent of children and young people had been consulted over their review and 59.4 per cent had attended their review.

The scrutiny of the 64 reviews for children looked after post implementation suggests the rate of consultation and attendance had fallen. Information on consultation had been recorded in 48 cases (75%) and on attendance in 50 cases (78.1%). The data revealed that two-thirds (66.6%) of children and young people had been consulted prior to the review and 47.7 per cent attended their review.

There were similar proportions of looked after children aged 10 years and over who were the subject of reviews included in both samples of social work records.

The findings suggest that when children are looked after social workers' recording of direct work with children remains high. However, the findings suggest a trend, since the implementation of the Integrated Children's System, for consultation and attendance of young people at review conferences to decline.

One factor in this decline may be the abandonment of specific materials to record consultation with children and young people (Grimshaw and Sinclair 1997). To avoid duplication and to enable practitioners to continue to use the consultation formats introduced with the Looking After Children materials or other existing materials no new consultation formats were introduced. However, informal discussions with practitioners suggest that since implementation these formats may not be being routinely used.

The information recorded on social work case records suggests that the implementation of the Integrated Children's System has affected the involvement of different groups of children unequally. Of particular concern is the lack of improvement, indeed the downward trend, in the involvement of looked after young people. The following part of this chapter focuses on the views of this group.

Young people's participation in plans and reviews: findings from the questionnaires

> Participation is a complex process. It should be on-going, neither excluding nor confined to crucial meetings. To be effective more than just the presence of young people at key meetings is required. (Triseliotis *et al.* 1995, p.209)

Profile of the young people returning questionnaires

The questionnaires for young people looked after were distributed through the link worker in the three authorities that had implemented the Integrated Children's System. However, despite considerable encouragement from the research team, responses were received from only one local authority, where 34 young people participated. All the young people had been involved in plans and reviews since the implementation of the Integrated Children's

System. The questionnaire covered a number of issues in-depth, including young people's involvement and experience of plans, reviews and decision making (see Appendix 1 for details).

The group was made up of equal numbers of boys and girls, whose ages spanned the adolescent years. Although most young people, regardless of their gender, were aged 14 years or more, a larger proportion of boys (29.4%) than girls (11.8%) were younger (see Table 6.1).

Table 6.1 Characteristics of the sample of young people

			Male	Female	Total
Age	10 or 11	Count	1	0	1
		% within gender	5.9%	0.0%	2.9%
	12 or 13	Count	4	2	6
		% within gender	23.5%	11.8%	17.6%
	14 or 15	Count	7	5	12
		% within gender	41.2%	29.4%	35.3%
	16 or over	Count	5	10	15
		% within gender	29.4%	58.8%	44.1%
Total		Count	17	17	34
		% within gender	100.0%	100.0%	100.0%

The young people lived in a variety of residences, although the majority were in residential care. Six were living with foster carers (four boys and two girls), 24 in a residential unit (equal numbers of boys and girls), one boy had been placed in a special school and three young women were living independently. Omitting those young people living independently, there was no link between the age of the young person and whether they were living with foster carers or in residential care.

The sample is biased towards young people living in residential care, a skew which probably reflects their greater accessibility (see Ward, Skuse and Munro 2005). The link worker responsible for distributing the questionnaire can email it to the care unit where it can be made readily available to all residents. In contrast, young people living in foster care must be contacted individually. Social workers told the research team that many fostered children frequently change their email address, making contacting them directly rather problematic. When emailed questionnaires did not result in a response there was no budget to fund social workers to carry out targeted visits to foster children, nor, it could be argued, would it have been appropriate.

Care plans

> The Care Plan is in two parts. Part One sets out the overall plan for the child which can only be changed at a statutory child care review. Part Two identifies what services are required to respond to the child's identified developmental needs. The Care Plan includes the personal education plan, health plan and plan for permanence. (Department of Health and Department for Education and Skills 2000–2005, Briefing Paper No. 5, p.5)

Twenty-seven young people (79.4%) reported that they knew about their care plan, a finding in line with the results of a 2007 consultation exercise involving 303 looked after young people from across England (Morgan 2007), and reflects the proportion (71%) found in a 2003 survey of 706 children and young people in public care (Timms and Thoburn 2003). The comparisons suggest little has changed with the implementation of the Integrated Children's System. Although social workers were responsible for telling 16 young people (59.2%) about their care plans, in eight cases (29.6%) the young person's carer had discussed the plan with them. Finally, in three cases young people only learnt about their care plan through attending a meeting where it had been discussed. Although the majority of young people knew about their care plan, nonetheless it was disquieting to discover that in seven cases (20.6%) young people did not have a clear understanding of the plan for their care.

The findings suggest that in this particular local authority it is not routine practice to provide young people with a copy of their care plan. In a third of cases (n=11) young people reported having been given a copy of their care plan, a rather lower proportion than the 53 per cent found in the English 2007 consultation exercise (Morgan 2007). Of the remaining 23 young people who did not have a copy of their plan half (n=12) reported that they would have liked to have been given a copy.

A key change introduced by the Integrated Children's System was separating the care plan into two parts. Part one of the plan covers:

- the overall aim of the plan
- where the young person will live

- the evidence to support the choice of placement
- any contingency plans
- the likely duration of the plan.

All the participating young people expressed a view about the issues they felt should be included in their care plan. Most (94.1%) thought the care plan should establish how long the young person will be looked after, where he or she will live, and when the residence period should end. However, among those young people who were aware of their care plan (n=27), a greater proportion (88.8%) knew how long they would be in care than knew where they would be living (70.3%).

Part two of the care plan covers:

- the young person's developmental needs (health, education, emotional and behavioural development, identity, family and social relationships, social presentation and self-care skills), details on how the needs will be responded to and the planned outcomes

- arrangements for contact with birth family members, relatives and other significant people

- the actions that the local authority will take, or facilitate on behalf of the parent(s)/birth family, to respond to the young person's needs and deal with the environmental factors that are affecting the identified need.

Part two also records the young person's views of the plan and the extent to which his or her wishes have been acted on, and the extent to which the wishes and views of other significant people have been obtained and acted upon. The identities of the agencies that have been consulted over the plan are recorded.

YOUNG PEOPLE'S VIEWS OF WHO SHOULD BE INVOLVED IN MAKING CARE PLANS

Young people identified a number of key people they thought should be involved in drawing up care plans for children and young people. In all cases they thought the young people themselves should be involved. In relation to professionals, most young people (91.2%) thought the social worker should be involved, and over a third thought a school representative should take part. A few young people mentioned other professionals such as doctors, nurses and children's rights workers.

Members of the birth family were seen as key participants to making care plans. Twenty-three young people (67.7%) thought birth parents should be involved, a third grandparents and some 30 per cent thought siblings should be involved. Finally, two young people mentioned the importance of involving either a trusted adult friend or a 'mate' whose role would be to support the young person. The importance of friends in supporting young people has been identified in earlier research (see, for example, Triseliotis et al. 1995).

YOUNG PEOPLE'S EXPERIENCE OF WHO WAS INVOLVED IN MAKING CARE PLANS

Young people's aspirations of who should be involved in making care plans did not always reflect their own reality. For example, not all the young people felt that they themselves had been involved in developing their care plan, indeed 11 (32.4%) reported a lack of involvement. It will be recalled that the scrutiny of social work case records showed the involvement of children and young people in care plans had not improved with the implementation of the Integrated Children's System.

When young people had been involved in making care plans most identified one or more people who had supported them in making their contribution. For example, 17 young people identified their social worker as the person who had involved them in care planning, 15 mentioned their carers, 10 mentioned attending a meeting where the care plan had been discussed, and 3 reported that their parents had discussed it with them.

Not all young people could recall those who had participated in the care planning process; 15 (44.1%) could not remember. However, when young people were able to recall the planning process, their expectations of the involvement of professionals generally coincided with reality.

In most cases (85.3%) young people reported that their social worker had been involved in drawing up their care plan. The perceived lack of social worker involvement in four cases could have a number of plausible explanations including sickness, a change in worker, or delegating the responsibility to another social services officer such as a family support worker. When it came to the involvement of representatives from schools or colleges, a fifth of young people reported their participation in developing their care plan.

In contrast to the involvement of professionals, the level of agreement between wishes and reality in relation to family members was poor. The birth parents of three young people were involved in the care plan and grandparents in only one case. No young person mentioned that a trusted friend had been involved. Because the Integrated Children's System requires practitioners, when drawing up a care plan, to explore the capacity of the birth family to meet the young people's needs and environmental factors that affect them, it should result in family involvement increasing. However, the findings would suggest that greater attention needs to be given to ensuring this happens.

YOUNG PEOPLE'S EXPERIENCE OF THE CONTENT OF THE CARE PLAN

The views of the young people suggest that they more readily agree with some aspects of the plan than others. For example, arrangements to see family members was an issue for 28 young people (82.4%) who thought it should be included.

> I want to see them more. (young woman aged between 14 and 15 in residential care)

Education was also seen as important; 26 young people (76.5%) wanted it included in the care plan.

> Plans for education, further education or higher education. (young woman aged 16 years who had just left the care of her foster parents to live independently)

Young people held differing opinions on whether other aspects of their lives should be covered. For example, 21 young people (61.8%) thought the plan should cover health issues and the same proportion felt family and social relationships should be included.

The sample was fairly evenly split when it came to more personal issues. For example, approximately half the sample (52.9%) felt the plan should cover how young people deal with their feelings (emotional and behavioural development) and the same number felt the plan should cover self-care skills.

Including sensitive issues, such as how young people see and feel about themselves (their identity) and how they look and behave towards other people (social presentation), was far less popular, factors wanted by 11 (32.4%) and 15 (44.1%) young people respectively.

Finally, some young people felt that the issues important to them were not always included in care plans. For example, one young man explained that his care plan should include 'more basic information that is relevant to me'.

Reviews

Government Guidance and Regulations (Department of Health 1991, Vol 3) supports the involvement by young people in review meetings. The Looking

After Children documentation included specific consultation papers that guided social workers and key workers through this process (Department of Health 1995c) and as discussed earlier no new documentation was introduced with the introduction of the Integrated Children's System. In the Guidance and Regulations the attendance of a young person for the whole of the meeting is taken as the norm, though part-attendance should also be considered. Consideration should be given to supporting the child during the meeting.

INVOLVING YOUNG PEOPLE IN PLANNING THEIR REVIEW

The Guidance and Regulations (Department of Health 1991, Vol 3) establishes an expectation that children and young people will be consulted, not only about their wishes and feelings in general, but also about specific aspects of the review such as the venue and who will attend. Although the scrutiny of social work records enabled the study to identify the rate of consultation it did not provide information about consultation over specific issues.

CONSULTATION ABOUT THE ORGANISATION OF REVIEW MEETINGS

The Government Guidance is clear about consulting children before deciding where to hold review meetings.

> The child should always be asked for his views about the venue. Meetings should be arranged at a place (and time) which will be the most likely to provide a setting and atmosphere conducive to the relaxed participation of all those attending. (Department of Health 1991, Vol 3, p.83, 8.18)

The Integrated Children's System supports practice in relation to consulting children and young people by requiring practitioners to record details of the consultation process including whether the young person was consulted in relation to the date, time, venue, agenda and participants.

Prior to the implementation of the Integrated Children's System consultation on the venue for the review was as likely to happen as not (Grimshaw and Sinclair 1997). The current research suggests little has changed. Fifteen young people (44.1%) recalled being consulted about the venue for their review, the same number thought they had not been asked and 4 young people could not remember.

A similar proportion felt that their views had been taken into consideration when the date for the review was decided. Sixteen young people

(47.1%) could recall being consulted about the date for their review meeting, 12 (35.3%) thought they had not been asked and 6 were unable to remember.

Social workers can be beguiled into thinking young people have been involved in decisions, such as the timing and venue for a review, because they were present during the discussion. However, being present does not mean being involved, as the young person quoted in Walker's study vividly illustrates.

> At the end of the review everybody gets their diary out to arrange the next meeting. But I don't have a diary so nobody asks me. (Walker 1999, p.38)

Government Guidance recommends that the attendance of the child and his or her parents at review meetings should be the norm rather than the exception. Invitations to other people should be done in consultation with the child or young person.

> The attendance of such people should always be discussed with the child before invitations are made and his views on their attendance obtained. (Department of Health 1991, Vol 3, p.83, 8.17)

The emphasis placed on consulting young people about who should attend their review meetings was in response to findings from a body of research on children and young people in contact with children's social care (Cleaver 1996).

> Several young people noted disapproval that people were present at reviews who they did not know and who they did not want to hear about the private concerns. (Triseliotis *et al.* 1995, p.209)

Research since the Children Act 1989 suggests that consultation remains perfunctory, with social workers preparing the invitation list without asking the young person whether there was anyone he or she wished to be included (Walker 1999). This resulted in some young people complaining that apparent strangers attended their reviews.

> There were people in my review that I don't even bloody know. (Walker 1999, p.38)

The present study suggests consultation over who should attend reviews may be showing signs of improvement. Half the young people reported that their social worker had discussed with them who should be invited to their review, 13 (38.2%) thought they had not been asked and the remaining 5 young people could not remember.

The Guidance (Department of Health 1991, Vol 3) advises that an agenda of the issues for discussion at the review should be circulated in advance to all those who are expected to attend, including the child. The reports of young people suggest less than half felt included in this process. Fifteen young people (44.1%) reported that the agenda for their review had been shared with them prior to the meeting, 14 (41.2%) thought that they had not had sight of it, and 5 couldn't remember.

PREPARING YOUNG PEOPLE FOR REVIEW MEETINGS

> The purpose of the review is to ensure that the child's welfare is safeguarded and promoted in the most effective way throughout the period he is looked after or accommodated. Progress in safeguarding and providing for the child's welfare should be examined and monitored at every review and the plan for the child amended as necessary to reflect any significant change. (Department of Health 1991, Vol 3, p.80, 8.1)

Preparation and communication before and after the meeting is essential to ensure that children and young people are able to participate meaningfully (Thomas and O'Kane 1998). However, interviews with a small group of young people, carried out prior to the implementation of the Integrated Children's System, found only a quarter could recall receiving any information about their forthcoming review (Grimshaw and Sinclair 1997). The findings from the current study suggest a marked improvement; three-quarters of young people (76.5%) reported having been provided with some written information that explained the purpose of review meetings.

The Guidance is clear that in preparing for the review the social worker should carry out a full consultation with all relevant individuals, including the young person, and prepare a written report for the meeting (Department of Health 1991, Vol 3).

Sixteen young people (47.1%) reported that social workers had discussed with them the issues they intended to include in their report to the review meeting. Moreover, 13 of these young people had also had an opportunity to comment on the social worker's written report prior to the meeting. For example, the social worker, carer or review chair had discussed the report with the young person prior to the meeting.

Many young people anticipate their review meetings with feelings of uncertainty and anxiety. Thorough preparation that includes talking young people through issues, such as who would be there, the layout of the meeting room, what people will wear, the role of the chair and other participants, the issues that would be discussed, the things they wanted to raise and how they could best do this, and the best and worst scenarios, has been shown in earlier research to be welcomed by both children and their parents and goes some way to alleviate their fears. In preparing young people for the meeting social workers should try to ensure the young person understands their own role and how attending the meeting may affect them emotionally (Cleaver and Freeman 1995; Corner, Rushforth and Shemmings 1999; Grimshaw and Sinclair 1997).

> Young people who felt they knew what would be discussed approached the meeting with greater calmness. (Grimshaw and Sinclair 1997, p.154)

The importance of preparing young people for review meetings and how this might encourage and support their involvement is summed up admirably in the following excerpt.

> The point about being better prepared is to be in a position to minimise surprise and thereby recapture the locus of control. This is the main purpose of preparing young people for meetings. Done well, it empowers them by minimising the unexpected and it helps them to express their own wishes and feelings. The extent to which the adults then listen and take any notice will determine whether the young person believes it was worth it or not. (Corner *et al.* 1999, p.109)

The Integrated Children's System supports consultation with young people; the young person's involvement in the review process and whether they had been consulted should be recorded on the system.

Previous research suggests that less than half (43.6%) of young people aged 11 to 16-plus were consulted prior to their review meeting (Grimshaw and Sinclair 1997). The current study suggests some improvement. For example, 22 young people (64.7%) reported that one or more professionals had talked to them about the issues that would be discussed at their forthcoming review. In the majority of cases the discussion had been between the young person and their social worker, carer or the review chair and in three cases young people reported that their parents had also talked them through what they thought would be discussed at the review meeting.

The other key issue in preparing young people for their forthcoming review is to ensure that they are supported in thinking through what they want to say. Unfortunately, fewer young people (47.1%) had been helped to prepare what they wanted to say and how best to do this at the meeting. For those who had received assistance, young people identified either their carers and/or their social workers as having worked with them on this task. In addition, five young people also recognised the support their parents had given them in preparing for the review meeting. Many young people had considerable support. For example, nine young people had help from a combination of their carers, social workers and parents. For one or two young people other professionals played a key role. For example, one young woman living in a residential unit noted that she had been helped to prepare what she wanted to say by the 'children's rights worker'.

Previous research suggests chairs take little part in preparing young people for their review and rarely meet before meetings even when they are strangers. Indeed, some young people may leave the meeting still not knowing the name of the chair (Grimshaw and Sinclair 1997). The reports of young people in the present study suggest that the Integrated Children's System has yet to affect this practice. Only ten young people (29.4%) met their review chair before the meeting.

ATTENDANCE AT REVIEW MEETINGS

> The attendance of the child and his parents at meetings to review the child's case will be the norm rather than the exception (subject to the reservations already expressed). (Department of Health 1991, Vol 3, p.83, 8.15)

Since the introduction of the Children Act 1989 children's attendance at reviews has been given greater priority by social workers. For example, one of the studies commissioned by the Department of Health to look at how the Act is working in England and Wales found that attendance of older children at review meetings was routine practice. The majority of 11 to 15 year olds, and nearly all 16 to 18 year olds, attended their meetings (Grimshaw and Sinclair 1997).

Young people

Although the attendance of young people at their review meetings appears to have become the norm, it would be presumptuous to assume that every child and young person wishes to be present. Formal meetings evoke feelings of stress and anxiety in many young people. They feel scrutinised and confronted with intrusive questions from adults who appear as strangers to them (Grimshaw and Sinclair 1997). Indeed, not all children and young people wish to be subjected to this and see it as the responsibility of their parents to represent their views at review meetings (Aldgate and Statham, 2001).

I like to know what's going to happen in the meeting. If there's lots of problems at the meeting…and if it's too pressurising, then I wouldn't want to go… I'd get someone else to go and talk for me. (Corner *et al.* 1999, p.107)

In the present study the majority of young people (91.2%) thought the young person should be present at review meetings. Of the three remaining young people, one had not answered the question while the two negative responses came from a young woman who attended her reviews and a young man who did not.

Parents

Government Guidance makes it clear that the local authority, where they consider it appropriate, should involve the child's parents in the review meetings. Previous research found that in approximately a third of cases (32.8%) mothers attended the reviews of children aged 11 years and over (Grimshaw and Sinclair 1997).

In the present study, although three-quarters of young people (76.5%) agreed with the principle that their parents should attend, reality was rather different. Less than half the young people (47.1%) reported that their parents usually attended their review meetings, suggesting that, although the rate of parental participation is improving in this authority, it remains low. In most cases young people expressed a wish for their non-attending parents to attend; nonetheless in three cases the opposite was true: the young people did not want parents who regularly attended to be present.

Carers

In addition to the parent and child, the child's carer should be invited. (Department of Health 1991, Vol 3, p.83, 8.17)

Research into children of all ages carried out prior to the Integrated Children's System suggests that 'foster carers and residential carers almost always attended reviews' (Grimshaw and Sinclair 1997, p.119). All the young people in the present study thought that their carers should attend review meetings. The rate of attendance for carers was generally high. When young people lived with foster carers in all cases young people reported that their carers routinely attended meetings. However, the attendance of link workers for the 24 young people in residential care was not as consistent; eight of these young people (33.3%) reported that their link worker did not routinely attend review meetings.

Relatives

> Other people with a legitimate interest in the child should also be invited if they have a contribution to make which indicates that they should take part in the discussions at the review meeting. (Department of Health 1991, Vol 3, p.83, 8.17)

Considerable research has shown that family members other than the child's parents can play a key role in the lives of children and young people who are looked after (Cleaver 2004). Nine young people thought members of their extended family, for example grandparents, aunts or uncles, should be invited to review meetings. In three cases this was reflected in practice. However, for the other six young people relatives did not routinely attend reviews. In contrast in two cases where young people did not want relatives to be invited, they were usually present. No data collected prior to the Integrated Children's System that explored the attendance of relatives could be identified to enable any comparisons to be made.

Educational representatives

Fourteen young people (41.2%) involved in the current study thought a representative from their school or other educational institution should attend. Young people's wishes did not always translate into reality; less than a third (32.4%) indicated that an educational representative routinely attended their review meeting. The rate of attendance is similar to that found in earlier research on a group of children of all ages where educational professionals attended 26 per cent of the reviews of looked after children (Grimshaw and Sinclair 1997).

It is of interest that there is considerable discordance between the group of young people who wanted educational representatives to attend and when attendance occurred. For example, in seven cases symmetry was found between wishes and reality, but in a further seven cases young people thought an educational representative should attend but no-one was routinely present, and in four cases a representative from education regularly attended reviews of young people who did not want them present.

Health representatives

Prior to the Integrated Children's System research found health professionals attended 14 per cent of the reviews of looked after children of all ages (Grimshaw and Sinclair 1997). This low rate of attendance is reflected by the reports of the young people in the present study; three young people (8.8%) reported their GP routinely attended their reviews.

It is of interest to note once again that young people's wishes did not always reflect reality. Only two young people thought their GP should attend review meetings but in neither case did this occur. Moreover, in three cases where GPs did attend review meetings the young people did not want them present.

ISSUES COVERED BY THE REVIEW

> 8.19 The primary matter for consideration of the review is the plan for the welfare of the child (under the general welfare duties placed on authorities by sections 22, 61 and 64 of the Children Act).

> 8.20 Schedule 2 of the Children Act 1989 provides a checklist of matters for consideration at the review which is not comprehensive or exclusive but sets the minimum requirements. (Department of Health 1991, Vol 3, p.84)

This checklist was translated into the review document in the Looking After Children materials (Department of Health 1995c). The main change introduced by the Integrated Children's System was to incorporate the issues on the checklist into the review of the young person's developmental dimensions, thus ensuring a detailed review of all aspects of the care plan.

> The Review Record commences with an evaluation of the child's developmental progress since the making of the plan or last review. It reviews the parents' and/or care givers' capacity to respond to the child's needs, and the family and environmental factors. The review considers the progress of the child, whether the planned outcomes have been achieved and any revisions required to the plan. (Department of Health and Department for Education and Skills 2000–2005, Briefing Paper No.5, p.6)

Previous research that explored young people's perceptions of reviews did not focus specifically on the issues that were covered. But a message that emerged from one study was that some young people were reluctant to talk about sensitive personal and family issues at reviews particularly in front of adults who appeared as strangers to them (Grimshaw and Sinclair 1997).

The questionnaire in the present study asked young people about the issues that were usually discussed at their review meetings and whether they thought this was appropriate. The response of one boy aged between 14 and 15 years who lived in a residential unit suggests total alienation from the review process. He reports that he doesn't usually attend reviews, does not want to attend, and when he does attend he 'don't listen and can't remember' what was discussed.

However, most young people in this authority did participate and were able to identify the issues that had been discussed at the meeting (see Table 6.2).

Table 6:2 Young people's perception of the rate at which issues were discussed at review meetings

Issue	Rate
Whether plans are working out as expected	96.9%
Young person's family	96.9%
School or college work	96.9%
Young person's health	96.7%
Recent changes in the young person's life	90%
Anticipated changes in the young person's life	90.6%
Day-to-day life with carers	87.5%
Young person's past	81.2%
Young person's feelings	75%
Young person's friends	54.8%

The findings suggest some issues were more likely to be routinely discussed at reviews than others. For example, the young person's family relationships, educational progress and health were nearly always raised while other issues such as feelings and their peer friendships were issues that were conspicuously less likely to be discussed.

This reluctance of the review meeting to discuss feelings and friendships reflects young people's views of what should be covered by the review. For example, where information was available it showed that over 90 per cent of young people felt it was appropriate for the meeting to discuss: whether plans were working out as expected, their day-to-day life with carers, and recent and anticipated changes to their lives. In addition the majority of young people (i.e. between 80 and 90%) were also content for the meeting to discuss their family and their school work, and 73.9 per cent were happy for their health to be discussed. More personal issues, however, such as young people's past, their friends and their feelings, were seen as 'off limits' by approximately half the group of young people who expressed a view.

However, recent studies of care leavers stress the importance of promoting young people's emotional and mental wellbeing as well as addressing practical needs (A National Voice 1999; Welsh Assembly Government 2005a). Moreover, research shows that many care leavers report feeling isolated and lonely after leaving care (Cleaver 1996).

DISAGREEMENTS BETWEEN YOUNG PEOPLE AND REVIEW MEMBERS

> Where disagreements arise in the course of the review process between the child and parents, the child and the responsible authority or the parents and the responsible authority, the responsible authority should make every effort to resolve these by explaining fully the reasons for their decisions. (Department of Health 1991, Vol 3, p.86, 8.25)

The Integrated Children's System supports this in that the formats are structured to enable a clear record to be made of any differences between the young person's views and those of professionals.

Young people find participating in review meetings difficult because they perceived them as being 'run by and for the adults' (Walker 1999). Research suggests a significant proportion of young people (61%) believe that review meetings listen to their views but are less sure they are able to influence the crucial decisions that affect their lives (Fletcher 1993).

> Most of the time I think they do listen, but they still make the decision that they want to make. (Fletcher 1993, p.50)

Young people feel that they are given a say in key decisions but voicing an opinion in official settings is difficult.

> The problem they felt was that this was often a formal right only, since meeting with several people made it hard to express themselves. (Triseliotis et al. 1995, p.210)

Moreover, when young people feel unable to express their views and believe their views are discounted and they are not treated with respect, this can alienate them from participating in any aspect of the assessment, planning or review process.

> Fundamental disagreements between professionals and a young person bred cynicism about reviews as such. (Grimshaw and Sinclair 1997, p.159)

The Integrated Children's System places great emphasis on preparing and supporting children and young people during reviews. The looked after review format provides space for the review chair to record how children are supported to contribute to their review and when relevant to record why this had not been done. This emphasis on support should enable children and young people to more readily voice their opinions about issues during the review process.

The findings from the young people's questionnaires suggest that the majority of them in this authority felt able to voice their views or dissent and in most cases issues were resolved satisfactorily. Sixteen of the 33 young people (48.5%) who attended their last review reported that things were said at review meetings which they thought were unfair or simply incorrect. Ten of these young people had brought the perceived inaccuracies or unfairness to the attention of the meeting. On the whole young people felt their initiative had led to some kind of resolution. Two young people said they had received an apology, four were provided with an explanation, and one young woman reported that 'we made a mutual agreement'. Only two young people felt that their protests had been ignored by the meeting. Finally, in one case the young man did not provide any information about how the meeting had responded to his comments.

Six young people reported that they had not brought the perceived unfairness or inaccuracy to the attention of the meeting. The reasons they gave for not doing so included: feeling that it didn't really matter (n=2); believing that their views would not be listened to (n=3); and one young man who feared that to voice his opinion would have resulted in an argument.

DECISION MAKING

Decision making is a crucial part of the planning and review process (Department of Health 1991). However, research suggests that decisions taken at reviews for looked after children were frequently unspecific.

> Exactly what was to be done was not specified because how to achieve the goal was sometimes unclear. (Grimshaw and Sinclair 1997, p.137)

The Integrated Children's System introduces greater clarity and specificity into the decision making process. For example, for a looked after young person with identified needs in relation to their emotional and behavioural development, the meeting should review what was done to meet these needs, the planned outcome and the actual outcome. The decision should be based on an analysis of this information and clearly recorded on the system.

Twenty-two young people (64.7%) could recall that the review meeting had resulted in decisions being taken. In a few cases where no decisions were taken the young person's report suggests the reason was outside the control of the meeting.

No decision due to court case. (young man aged between 12 and 13 years)

Decisions that were taken by review meetings included those about the young person's current placement, education and work, contact with family and future living arrangements, as the following quotations illustrate.

Current placement

I would stay in my present permanent foster placement. (boy aged between 10 and 11 years)

To remain at the home until a new long-term placement turns up or when I'm 16 go into independent living. (young woman aged between 14 and 15 years)

Education and work

That I stay with my present foster carers that I will change schools. (girl aged between 12 and 13 years)

To complete a college course. (young man aged over 16 years)

Family contact

See Mum once a month with Nana. (boy aged between 12 and 13 years)

More effort into family contact. (young man aged over 16 years)

Future living arrangements

The plan to return home. (girl aged between 12 and 13 years)

That I would be living independently in six months. (young woman aged over 16 years)

Twenty-one of the 22 young people who could remember the review meeting taking a decision that affected them understood why it had been taken and most (n=18) agreed with the decision. Moreover, in all but one case the young person was able to identify those responsible for carrying out particular decisions.

When review meetings take decisions about children or young people the timescale for implementing the decision should also be decided. Just over half the young people (59.1%) were able to recall if a date had been set by which the decision should be carried out.

Young people's views on the results of decisions made at the review meetings were varied. For example, 12 young people (35.3%) held very positive views, believing that decisions taken at the meeting were implemented always, or most of the time. A further 15 young people (44.1%) were fairly positive about review decisions, believing they were realised some of the time. However, seven young people (20.6%) held very jaundiced views, believing that decisions made at review meetings seldom or never came to fruition.

NOTIFICATION OF THE RESULTS OF THE REVIEW

> Regulation 7(3) requires that the child, his parent, others with parental responsibility and other persons considered appropriate are notified of the result of the review and decisions taken in consequence of the review... The notification of the result of each review meeting should be a written summary of the main points of the written report of the review which makes clear who is responsible for implementing decisions arising from the review and the relevant time-scales. (Department of Health 1991, Vol 3, p.85, 8.22 and 8.23)

The child or young person's looked after review included in the Integrated Children's System has two parts. The first is the social worker's report which provides details of the young person's needs and circumstances, the actions and services provided, and the planned outcomes (identified during the assessment and previous review). The report then details the findings from the present review in relation to the young person's progress, reviews the care plan, the placement arrangements and agreements, and any contact arrangements.

The second part is a summary of the discussions and decisions taken at the review. It is written by the review chair at the end of the review process and a copy or summary of the decisions should be provided to all participants.

The reports from the young people included in the present study suggest in this particular local authority it is not routine practice to provide them with a copy of the review. Eighteen young people (52.9%) received a copy of the first part of their review and only 14 (41.2%) received a copy of the second part.

Being provided with a copy of the review document itself may not be appropriate for all young people; as one 16-year-old young woman pointed out, 'It's too long.' Nonetheless, young people need to understand and have a record of the decisions that have been taken, the timescales and who will be responsible for carrying them out. A more accessibly written report that provides the key information would be welcomed. For example, one young man (aged between 10 and 11 years) wanted 'a short simple report that is clear and easy to understand'.

Summary points

- The examination of social work files suggests social workers are more conscientious in recording the participation and involvement of some groups of children and young people than others.

- Recording the views and involvement of children at child protection conferences and reviews has shown some improvement with the implementation of the Integrated Children's System but remains uncommon.

- Although children looked after are more likely to be involved in plans and decisions that affect them, the introduction of the Integrated Children's System has had little impact. This lack of improvement was also identified when scrutinising looked after reviews.

- In contrast, the implementation of the Integrated Children's System has improved the extent to which young people are involved in Pathway Plans.

- The findings from the questionnaires, completed by 34 young people looked after in one pilot authority, indicate that most were aware of their care plan both prior to and after the introduction of the Integrated Children's System.

- Young people were generally content with the degree of professional involvement in their care plans but wanted parents and family members to play a greater role.

- Young people held decided opinions on the issues that care plans should cover. Although the majority thought plans should cover living arrangements, education, health and family and social relationships, there was less consensus on more sensitive issues such as identity and social presentation.

- The findings suggest that informing young people about their reviews has improved; three-quarters of young people reported receiving some written information explaining the purpose of their forthcoming review. However, less than half the young people had been helped to prepare what they wanted to say at the meeting, and less than a third had met their review chair prior to the meeting.

- Young people wanted a greater involvement of their parents and other members of the family in their reviews. The findings suggest that although parental attendance is less than young people would wish it has improved.

- The matters considered at reviews were generally accepted by young people. However, personal issues such as the young person's past, their friends and their emotions and feelings were not always seen as appropriate subjects for discussion in such a forum.

- The Integrated Children's System introduces greater clarity and specificity into the decision making process which appears to be having a positive impact on practice. However, despite the greater specificity of decisions not all young people were confident that decisions would be implemented, indeed a fifth were very cynical.

- Approximately half the young people had been provided with a copy of their review report. This method of informing young people of the results of their review, however, is not always appropriate and some young people expressed a wish for a shorter and more accessible report.

Chapter 7

Use of Information Technology

Introduction

It is important to understand the difference between the Integrated Children's System and an information technology (IT) system. The Integrated Children's System is

> a conceptual framework, practice discipline and business process that helps front-line social care staff undertake work with children and families in a systematic manner. It should help them and their managers to collect and use case information systematically, efficiently and effectively. (Department for Education and Skills 2005a)

It is not itself an IT system but 'the volume and complexity of information… require that the Integrated Children's System is underpinned by Information Technology (IT)' (*ibid.*).

The Integrated Children's System is underpinned by the Core Information Requirements, a set of specifications which aim to identify all the information required for the delivery of children's social care services (Department of Health 2001b). These include a Process Model (Department for Education and Skills 2003c), which maps the core business processes of children's social care services, and a Data Model, which codifies the data items identified in the Process Model (Department for Education and Skills 2003d) and their logical inter-relationships. These two models 'should not be considered prescriptive in themselves', but a system which does not contain all the information requirements they outline 'is unlikely to support compliance' (*ibid.*). In addition, the then Department for Education and Skills (now the Department for Children, Schools and Families) provided an Outputs Model which describes how information, once recorded and stored in an IT system, can be retrieved and used in social work practice (Gatehouse, Statham and Ward 2004a and 2004b).

The practice component of the Integrated Children's System comprises the set of 26 exemplars intended to demonstrate how core information about a child should be gathered by professionals undertaking the key social care processes necessary for successful case management. While the core data requirements must be met, the exemplars themselves 'are not mandatory in the sense that they must be followed to the letter. They are examples of organising the information on and about children in need for particular purposes in order to manage the case' (Department for Education and Skills 2005b).

Finally, the Integrated Children's System is first and foremost a practice system for social services. However much it may help and promote multi-agency working, it is not in itself a multi-agency system. The Integrated Children's System is not the same as the Common Assessment Framework (CAF), though the latter should 'take account of the structure of the ICS' (Department for Education and Skills 2005a). Also, 'it is important to clearly distinguish Integrated Children's System from the Information Sharing Index (IS Index) that is currently under development. The former entails the electronic recording of detailed case information for children receiving social services. The IS Index will hold information on all children' (*ibid.*) The IS Index is now being developed as Contact Point in England.

The most succinct statement of the various requirements for information systems supporting the Integrated Children's System is set out in the circular, Integrated Children's System: A Statement of Business Requirements (Department for Education and Skills 2005a; Welsh Assembly Government 2005b). This statement forms the benchmark against which information technology used to support the Integrated Children's System can be evaluated. (For a full list of supporting documentation see Department of Education and Skills 2007.)

Use of IT to support the Integrated Children's System in the pilot authorities

This chapter considers the ways in which the pilot authorities developed their information technology to support the operation of the Integrated Children's System and draws on three sources of information:

- structured questionnaires covering both the development process and the functionality of the resulting IT systems; these were

completed by the Integrated Children's System Project and IT Lead
Officers in each authority

- questionnaires relating to IT usage and training (completed by 46
  social work managers and practitioners), although the findings
  from these data have been covered in more detail in Chapter 4

- field trips to each of the authorities to audit their IT systems based
  on using the Statement of Business Requirements (Department for
  Education and Skills 2005a); the field trips were conducted in
  2005 and involved an examination of the IT system in each
  authority and interviews with key staff.

Although the Unitary Authority did not implement their system in time for
the research team to assess its impact on social work recording practice, it
was possible to capture data on the system itself. As a result this chapter is
based on the experience of the four pilot authorities and identifies some of
the issues which have wider implications for all local authorities as they
begin to implement the Integrated Children's System. A more detailed
and technical discussion can be found in English Pilots, ICS IT Systems:
Technical Report (Department of Health and Department for Education and
Skills 2000–2005, Briefing Paper No.7).

The IT requirements of pilot authorities

In order to participate in the research authorities agreed to implement the
Integrated Children's System in an electronic format. Authorities were free to
develop their own IT solutions, but their system had to have the following
features:

- It had to be based on the Core Information Requirements and
  Process Models (Department of Health 2001b).

- Although the way in which information was recorded and
  structured within the authority's IT system could vary, the
  information produced for children and families and other
  professionals as printed outputs of the system had to be consistent
  with the exemplars.

- The system had to allow single data entry.

Single data entry

The Integrated Children's System exemplars contain many pieces of information which are repeated on successive documents. These include both basic details of the child concerned (e.g. name, address, date of birth, ethnicity, case or referral number) and larger pieces of contextual information. For example, the details of a child's plan are repeated in the review.

Nothing causes practitioners more annoyance than being obliged to write down or type the same information repeatedly. In a database system this should be unnecessary, since both screen forms and printed reports are merely 'masks' or templates through which the same data, stored once and in only one place, is viewed or presented. Techniques of 'database normalisation', known as Codd's Rules (Codd 1970), are now widely implemented, precisely to avoid the duplication and inaccuracies which arise when the same data is stored in more than one place. The Integrated Children's System was designed to facilitate the transfer of information between different exemplars and therefore single data entry was viewed as essential for its successful implementation. If implementation of the Integrated Children's System is also to lead to improvements in the use of information by children's services, it is also important that all information captured be treated as data.

> The system should be capable of storing ICS exemplar data items electronically... Sections on data entry forms should correspond to coded data or text fields that are stored in the back office database. Different outputs should be defined as combinations of coded fields that make up a template for the output. (Department for Education and Skills 2004)

The situation in the pilot authorities prior to Integrated Children's System implementation

One of the criteria for selecting the four pilot local authorities was the extent to which their practitioners had access to computers, the degree of IT support available and the capacity of software to enable information to be analysed for management purposes. The pilot authorities were chosen because they were, on the whole, considered to be 'ahead of the game', so it is likely that the situation may be considerably less favourable in many other authorities in England and Wales.

Existing hardware provision

At the start of the pilot (2002–2003) all four authorities already had existing high speed networks. However, these did not always extend to all users. For example, in the Welsh Local Authority, seven outlying offices had only a dial-up modem connection to the main network. The significance of this constraint has been noted in other studies, where it was also apparent that staff at the centre are often unaware of the difficulties experienced in outlying offices (Gatehouse and Ward 2003; Gatehouse *et al.* 2004a).

The ratio of staff to computers varied. The London Borough was the only authority where every field social worker had a personal computer. In the other pilot authorities computers were shared between two or more practitioners. The majority of practitioners polled (95.4%) reported that they had ready access to a computer. The specification of the computers on the network was also highlighted as posing problems for the Integrated Children's System implementation teams. The Welsh Local Authority stated that the computers which were in place were of varying specification and running a wide range of different (MS Windows) operating systems.

Who does the recording?

There were considerable differences between the pilot authorities in the allocation of detailed case recording work (especially new referrals, case notes and assessments) between practitioners and administrative staff. Initially this appeared to be primarily a hardware and secondly a skills problem which would be resolved in favour of practitioner recording once every social worker had a dedicated computer and adequate IT and typing skills. It became clear, however, that the picture was more complex.

The Welsh Local Authority, for instance, which experienced great difficulties in recruiting social workers, had some years earlier taken an explicit decision to have as much data recording as possible undertaken by administrative staff, in order to free social work practitioners to work directly with service users. At the same time it provided a much higher proportion of administrative to practitioner posts than is the norm, and had made considerable efforts to minimise any delays caused by passing hand-written forms to administrators for electronic recording.

Elsewhere there were marked differences in work patterns, culture and attitude to recording even among teams within a single authority. It may be relatively easy to directly record initial referrals, except where the volume of contacts or a sluggish IT system makes this impractical. On the other hand, much of the information for core assessments and from visits is accrued in the field where use of a computer, even a laptop, is impractical. Practitioners varied in their approach to recording this information depending on their IT skills, the quality of the IT system and their familiarity and access to it. Some practitioners were happy to record case notes and core assessments on an IT system, whilst others recorded on paper in the first instance and passed their manuscript to an administrator for electronic recording.

Existing electronic information systems

All the authorities had an existing electronic information system at the start of the pilot. This usually consisted of a client index database containing basic information (for example, name, address, date of birth) and some means of managing the processes of contact, referral and case allocation. Where forms, such as those for Looking After Children and the Assessment Framework, were included, these were usually Word (or equivalent) templates and were to some extent managed by, but not truly integrated into, the database. None appeared to have fully integrated their electronic information systems into the everyday working of all front-line staff. The Unitary Authority commented:

> The main customer index was and remains…available to all over the network but is very little used by the majority of Children's Services staff. Its functionality has never been fully exploited.

The lack of an integrated IT system was reflected in the experiences of practitioners; only half reported using a computer to access information about children on a daily basis. A quarter said that they accessed information about children on a monthly basis, or not at all. The level of practitioner data entry was similar. About two-thirds of practitioners claimed to use computers to key in data, but, of these, 40 per cent stated that this was not a daily task.

Other studies have demonstrated that for many users, especially practitioners, IT systems are not a source of, but a deposit for, information. They regard the systems as being, essentially, bureaucratic recording systems, into which information must be entered, because administrators, managers or inspectors require it, but not as being the means of retrieving the information they need to manage the cases of children for whom they are responsible (Gatehouse *et al.* 2004a and 2004b). Prior to the implementation of the Integrated Children's System, this was also the case in the pilot authorities.

Developing IT to support the Integrated Children's System

All four pilot authorities had plans for continued IT upgrade and development in place before the Integrated Children's System implementation. None had the flexibility or resources required to implement the Integrated Children's System fully and, without exception, they all required substantial overhaul once the nature of the Integrated Children's System became apparent.

General issues relating to IT

In developing their electronic solutions to the Integrated Children's System the pilot authorities encountered a number of issues, which brought into sharp relief the questions which must be addressed in any IT system for children's social care.

First, the number of client records is comparatively small, but the amount of information stored on each client is very large (the Data Model has over 7000 separate data items which potentially could be recorded for each child). Second, the number and rate of transactions (changes or additions to existing records) is low, but the amount of detail and variability in each transaction is high. Third, much of the information consists not of quantities and classifications but of free text to describe judgements, opinions, statements and varied narratives of events and characteristics.

Thus an appropriate IT system for children's social care must:

- be capable of storing, presenting, retrieving and formatting large volumes of text data
- include search functions able to search on many different data items and also within text strings
- provide many different screen and report formats, for entering, viewing and printing information; the design of these formats needs to ensure that associated information is presented in clear, easily-navigable layouts
- include reports which present and summarise information within a child's record (e.g. a chronology) and across a group of children (e.g. siblings), and can present textual information as well as numeric aggregations
- enable users to define filters to view or print specified sub-sets of records without the need for professional IT assistance

- have a user-interface which follows closely the working processes used by practitioners and enables users to navigate the system and locate and juxtapose disparate pieces of information easily and intuitively both within a child's record and across the records of different children.

The experience of the pilot authorities suggests that the combination of effective search facilities and good screen formats will determine the extent to which users, especially social work practitioners, use an electronic system, rather than paper case files, as their preferred source of information on the cases for which they are responsible.

Multi-agency issues

Although the Integrated Children's System is not *per se* a multi-agency system, it is being implemented at a time when new multi-agency initiatives are being widely promoted in both England and Wales as part of the Every Child Matters and Change for Children policy initiatives.

This means that developers of IT systems cannot confine their attention solely to the requirements of children's social care. In addition to developing the technology necessary to implement the Integrated Children's System they need to take into account both practice- and IT-based initiatives for information sharing. These include the Common Assessment Framework, the Electronic Social Care Record and information sharing initiatives, such as the Information Sharing Index, the National Programme for Information Technology (NPfIT) in the NHS and various other e-Government initiatives; and the numerous local initiatives and projects of local authorities and their partner agencies. IT systems to support the Integrated Children's System will need to be compliant or at least capable of communicating with some or all of these and to be able to evolve as new projects come online.

A further multi-agency issue was that, at the time of the research, none of the pilot authority's IT systems allowed documents received from other agencies to be scanned into the child's electronic file. As a consequence, practitioners had to manage two sets of files: an electronic one which contained the information created by their own agency and a paper file which contained information received from other agencies. However, the pilot authorities saw the Integrated Children's System as central to the development of an electronic social care record where all information about a child would be held electronically. To try and manage this dilemma the pilot authorities developed policies which stressed that the electronic file was to be used as the primary source for information; the location of any paper records had to be clearly noted.

Text handling

As mentioned above IT systems for children's social care have to store and manage large quantities of free text. Modern computers and database systems are almost entirely indifferent as to whether a given data item is a single 'bit' representing a True/False value, a double-byte representing a number or a long string of bytes which may contain whole words, sentences, paragraphs or volumes of text. Thus items such as the social worker's summary of the child's attachment needs can be a data item just as the child's date of birth, gender or number of siblings.

The three authorities that successfully implemented their IT system within the timescale of the research piloting were exploring how best to store free text in the exemplars as data. This involved having to clarify how free text could be collected and collated, repeated where appropriate, set alongside other similar data, searched, categorised, analysed, presented and disseminated.

Individual child records and 'cloning'

The Integrated Children's System stresses the importance of assessment, planning, intervention and review for each child and this requires separate records to be created for each individual. However, in practice there may be data that are common to all the children in a family. For example, although individual children may be affected differently by the impact of issues which impair their parents' parenting capacity, the issues themselves may be the same. Pilot authorities reported that it was important to have a facility which enabled practitioners to copy or 'clone' information, where this was common to more than one child, rather than requiring them to record the same information several times.

However, they also stressed that this facility should be carefully managed as unrestricted cloning may encourage poor practice and a failure to properly identify the needs of the individual child. An intelligent IT system may permit cloning, while clearly identifying the cloned data and prompting users to add child-specific details.

Workflow management systems

The work processes which social workers undertake follow particular paths which vary, depending on the decisions made at each stage. These processes are mapped in detail in the Core Information Requirements Process Model and its accompanying process flow diagrams (Core Information Requirements) which locate the various exemplars beside the process where each should be completed. IT systems which support the Integrated Children's System readily lend themselves to the inclusion of workflow management.

Workflow management guides practitioners through the various stages that are involved in any practice process. It ensures that, when undertaking a social work process, practitioners are provided with the appropriate information available from the authorities' IT systems. It assists practitioners in identifying any further information and actions which may be necessary to complete the practice process and can support front-line managers by identifying when, and whether, key actions and information have been undertaken and recorded.

All of the pilot authorities included workflow management in their IT solutions to the Integrated Children's System. Their experiences indicated that the following issues need to be taken into account when developing such management systems.

- Workflow systems are dependent on clear business processes. These need to reflect the requirements of the Data and Process models, but to be useful to social work practitioners they must also closely match locally developed processes and systems. The pilots reported that mapping local business processes was extremely time consuming and, although they welcomed the opportunity to clarify and, in many cases, simplify existing processes, they had underestimated the preparatory work involved. This had a significant impact on their implementation plan and budget.

- IT systems which incorporate workflow management must be flexible enough to respond to the complexity encountered by practitioners in their day-to-day practice. Workflow systems which are too inflexible to allow users to do what they need to do can be frustrating and counter-productive. Such systems tend to be disliked by their users, who resort or revert to their own 'parallel' systems (usually lists stored as documents or spreadsheets and unconnected in any way with the main IT system), devise ways of 'fooling the system' to evade unrealistic constraints or avoid using them altogether. The existence of such multiple, parallel systems leads to poor data quality and undermines user confidence in the 'official' system (Gatehouse and Ward 2003).

- A final issue with any workflow management implementation is that processes and connections between processes are constantly evolving. Any Integrated Children's System IT system with workflow management at its core will require modification from time to time to keep up with these changes. Planning, budget and staff resources for such modifications need to be in place otherwise the IT system will become progressively less useful.

Level of functionality

The experiences of the pilot authorities in developing and implementing their solutions to the Integrated Children's System informed the development of the statement of business requirements for the Integrated Children's System (Department for Education and Skills 2005a; Welsh Assembly Government 2005b). The business requirements set out the level of functionality which IT solutions to the Integrated Children's System must meet.

Although not part of the original research requirements the pilot authorities agreed to have their IT systems audited against this detailed specification. The audit was used to inform the then Department for Education and Skills and Welsh Assembly Government on the level of support that other authorities were likely to require to meet the specification set out in the business requirements. The findings of the audit were used to develop English Pilots, ICS IT Systems: Technical Report (Department of Health and Department for Education and Skills 2000–2005, Briefing Paper No.7). This section reports the key findings of the audits. Quotations (direct or paraphrased) from the statement of business requirements appear indented.

System accessibility

Each front-line staff member will have dedicated access to a computer as and when necessary to undertake case recording and case management.

Three out of the four pilot authorities responded in the affirmative, though in one the workers in family and residential centres had to share computers. The fourth authority had only one computer per two social workers, but intended to purchase laptops for all their social workers.

Until each social worker has dedicated access to a computer, it is unlikely that they will regularly and routinely use it for accessing information. They might sometimes be willing to wait until a machine is free to do some recording, but their need to retrieve information is usually immediate – for instance while they are responding to a telephone enquiry. If the electronic system does not meet that need, they will not rely on it, preferring case files, their own notes, lists and parallel information systems.

While network access was generally adequate, two authorities reported that it was not available to their emergency duty teams (EDTs). Adequate information provision is essential for the EDT function. Commonly problems arise where EDTs are located outside council offices or are delegated to other providers.

Outputs for social workers

> Having entered information, staff will be able to output (to print or screen as appropriate) information in a convenient and concise format.

At the time of the research none of the IT systems in the pilot authorities provided practitioners with the facility to select and print off the essential details of a case drawn from different forms/data input screens. Yet selective, summary reports are extremely useful, for instance, when leaving the office to make a visit, attend court, or take part in a multi-agency discussion. Such a report would have probably formed the first section of every child's paper case file, being regularly exchanged for a new, updated version whenever basic details were changed. The facility to produce them would help both to reinforce the idea of the electronic record as the definitive source of correct, up-to-date information about the child and to provide the visible link between the paper and electronic records. All such reports should be automatically dated.

> Front-line staff will be able to see on a computer screen basic summary information (name, address, case number, legal status) basis for being looked after/supervision/other orders, registrations, family members, relevant adults (including professionals) and significant others, with contact details, etc., on each child for whom they have responsibility.

The absence of a personal details report led to an enquiry as to whether the screens themselves were absent or hard to access. The findings suggest that in some systems 'personal details' screens were awkward to view and navigate, and in many cases the personal details were not completed. A key factor was that personal details screens tended to be filled in at the point of referral, when information was often still incomplete. As details emerged in the course of subsequent assessments, visits and routine casework, there was no clear process step for recording them except, possibly, via the Chronology, but this in turn tended not to be well implemented. This is an important finding that should inform implementation in other authorities.

Personal details screens and reports might also usefully include summary texts from the most recent referral, assessment, plan and review; and the date and a one-line summary of the most recent visit, case note and supervision decisions (Gatehouse *et al.* 2004b). Together, these items constitute the bare minimum that someone picking up the case without prior knowledge or full recall of it would need to know to understand the child's current status. It would enable a colleague covering for the child's allocated social worker to pick up and act on the case appropriately; similarly it would form a quick introduction for a discussion at case conference or supervision. None of the systems within the pilot authorities provided this option to practitioners.

Case notes

Case notes or detailed records are an important part of social work practice. They provide a mechanism for reflective practice, support and analysis and decision making (Walker *et al.* 2003a). All the information systems in use in the pilot authorities provided the means of recording and printing case notes, but seldom related them to the other records in the system. Some practitioners complained about the poor retrieval and output facilities for case notes. They wanted to be able to sort and filter notes by child, type and date and print full notes or lists of notes, with just the date, type and headline shown (see Gatehouse *et al.* 2004a). None of the pilot authorities appeared to have succeeded in resolving this issue at the time of the research.

Chronologies

> Front-line staff and managers will be able to access a chronology of key events in the life of each child...automatically updated...historic information will be entered into the system as it is discovered through assessment and other case activity.

The Victoria Climbié Inquiry (Cm 5730 2003) recommended: 'Directors of social services must ensure that every child's case file includes, on the inside of the front cover, a properly maintained chronology.'

The chronology proved to be the most complex component to develop in authorities' IT systems. In part this was due to the fact that authorities had focused on the exemplars in developing their system. Since the chronology was dependent upon information from other exemplars, it tended to be the last element of the system to be developed.

The difficulties in developing chronologies also reflected differences in understanding between IT developers and practitioners of what constituted a chronology. For IT developers a chronology was often simply a record of all activity recorded on the system in relation to a child or young person. However, an undifferentiated list will not support practitioners to identify patterns or understand the immediate and cumulative impact of life events on the child or young person. The IT needs to enable practitioners to develop a chronology which can bring together key information that may be relevant to the circumstances of the child and the current concern. A critical feature will be the capacity for practitioners to apply professional judgement in selecting the events that should be included. None of the pilot authority systems had this level of functionality for developing a chronology.

Reminders

> Front-line staff and managers will be alerted when key events (assessments, reviews, etc.) are approaching, due or overdue... The system will record 'flags' that help to safeguard and promote the welfare of children, including adults who may constitute a threat... These 'flags' will give rise to alerts that are outputs...

All four pilot authorities had developed some form of automatic notification to help safeguard and promote the welfare of children. For example, the systems in two authorities incorporated alerts for assessments and reviews, and warnings or flags to highlight special needs or risks. Another authority had a single text-box for 'dangers/risks/issues' which displayed on the 'Personal Details' screen of the child's record, while the remaining authority displayed a 'Risk Assessment Completed' flag on the Referral and Information Record.

Outputs for team managers

The Business Requirements for team and other managers include the ability to see a list of all children assigned to the team and any unallocated cases. All four pilot authorities met this requirement. Similarly, managers should receive the appropriate reminders about reviews, assessments and other processes pending (met in two authorities). The systems in three of the pilot authorities enabled managers to access screens which showed the details and status of an individual child, which tasks are outstanding and dates of the latest visit, contact arrangements, and so on. In the remaining authority this was possible only by working through a number of screens.

> Team managers will be able to output basic statistics for the activity of their team...

A scrutiny of the IT systems showed that at the time of the study only one pilot authority had fully developed this facility; the other three were working towards this end.

The reports of team managers also suggested that during supervision meetings they did not routinely use and/or review the computer records of children allocated to the social worker. Team managers are the bridge between front-line work with individual children and the organisation of children's social care. Using the IT system in supervision sessions will help them to monitor the workloads and activity of practitioners as well as to gain an understanding of how each social worker is using information and the extent to which the information system is serving the practitioners' needs. If team managers either cannot or do not examine the electronic records of children, they cannot monitor whether these records are complete and up-to-date and support practitioners' use of the system.

Management information

> Senior managers will be able to output basic statistics of activity and outcome (performance indicator) data for all teams...and for the...authority.

In general, the management information facilities were not yet well developed and usually required intervention by IT or business information staff to produce and customise the requisite outputs. The process of enabling managers to monitor their own performance and that of their teams and sections was only just beginning.

None of the four pilot authorities' systems could easily produce statistics on non-acute services. Apart from some Child and Adolescent Mental Health Services (CAMHS) referrals, referrals to non-acute services were not recorded in a structured way: the decision to refer might be recorded in a child's plan, but the actual referral would be recorded, if at all, in a case note or through correspondence. Without structured information about access and take-up of such services it is not possible to calculate the costs of provision for children in need.

> Children whose outcome(s) fall outside a performance indicator standard will be readily identifiable...

Only one authority used their IT system to routinely produce exception reports alongside its management statistics.

Central to both the production and ownership of management information is the question 'Who is able to compile performance data and identify exceptions?' Practice varied between the authorities, ranging from administrative staff and business information units to team managers and all users. Previous research suggests that, unless staff have the tools to analyse their own work, reports are often not 'owned' by the teams and sections whose work is described and judged by the statistics (Gatehouse *et al.* 2004b).

Data quality is of central importance, not only for the management of individual cases and the safety and welfare of the children, but also for the confidence staff have in the validity of performance measurements. In general, administrative staff had the job of validating records and checking for errors. Several combined this with case audits involving both electronic and paper records and conducted by team or service managers.

Cross-views

> For each child it will be possible to list the services...received... And conversely, for each service...to list the children currently and historically served.

This view of the data is termed a 'cross-view'. Previous research suggests that such outputs are accorded low priority, that the work of family placement, fostering and adoption teams is poorly supported by their IT systems and, in general, that available data is not easily retrieved to facilitate the planning and commissioning of services (Gatehouse and Ward 2003; Gatehouse *et al.* 2004a). Three pilot authorities could produce cross-views for foster placements and carers, although in one access was restricted to administrative staff. As noted above, data on non-acute services was seldom formally recorded.

Filtering

Pilot authorities were asked whether their system could identify the children due to sit statutory assessment tests such as SATs or GCSE examinations. Only two authorities had this capability; the others could do it, 'but only if a report template was set up'.

This response reveals another limitation of the information systems at that time: any kind of filtering (selection) of data is normally possible only as part of a report and no user-friendly interface was provided for practitioners to construct their own queries to perform such filtering on the fly. The absence of this facility is a factor in making such systems appear to be static repositories of historic information rather than sources from which valuable data about an ongoing case can be retrieved.

Integrated Children's System exemplars

> Information required for each of the key processes for responding to children in need…will be held electronically using the content of the appropriate ICS exemplar.

With the exception of one or two exemplars that were still awaiting full implementation (see above), this requirement was being met in all four pilots, and all except one stated that they could separately access all the information contained in an exemplar without calling up the whole.

Security

Three of the four pilot systems provided some degree of security and the remaining authority was in the process of developing their security system. However, for the most part this was confined to limiting who could make changes rather than who had access to the information. Having too little security can be as great a problem as having too much, as staff will be reluctant to record information if they fear that it might be visible to staff in other teams, sections or agencies.

Well-secured information systems tend to implement 'user-level' or 'profile-based' security which can specify down to the level of the individual data item exactly what may be read, created, edited or deleted by each user, depending on a profile of who they are (e.g. post, team, seniority). There is, however, a trade-off between security and practicality. The profiles will be different for each authority and therefore a management console must be included to enable a system administrator to configure the security profile of each user. The system administrator needs to understand not only the technical details of the IT system, but the practical needs and structures of children's services. The role of system administrator is often delegated to the IT department, where staff may not understand the practice requirements and organisation of the service, let alone the details of client consent and confidentiality.

Multi-agency provision

Adding multi-agency facilities to the Integrated Children's System IT system is one of the most challenging tasks of the IT development. None of the pilot authorities' IT systems was fully integrated with data systems in other agencies. However, two of the authorities had established one-way information flows with specific external agencies.

- The Welsh Local Authority was able to present users within some schools customised read-only data screens within the Integrated Children's System IT system itself. These users could log on and interrogate the Integrated Children's System within the limits set by social services. This access had been extremely well received and the authority had received requests for similar facilities from GPs, health visitors, housing and the police. Work was under way with health and police IT departments to try and establish a two-way flow of information between their systems.

- The Shire County had established a one-way electronic transfer of information from the education database into their Integrated Children's System IT system.

Enabling practitioners from other agencies to log on as users of the children's social care system is one approach to aid information sharing. Setting up automatic electronic information exchange is a different one. Both approaches require complex issues of information governance, data protection and technical security to be resolved. Exploring different models of extending access to the Integrated Children's System to professionals from a range of disciplines has been identified as one of the key tasks to be undertaken at government level to improve the identification of risk and ultimately the outcomes for children in care (Cm 6932 2006).

Summary of functionality

The findings suggest that the pilot authorities' IT systems were meeting the recording requirements of the Integrated Children's System and the statistical reporting needs of service and performance managers. However, the limited availability of information outputs meant systems, at the time of the research, were not able to meet fully the operational needs of practitioners, administrative staff and team managers for managing the complex cases of individual children. In this context 'outputs' refer to information which is retrieved by and/or presented to the user in whatever form, whether in lists and forms on the computer screen, electronic messages (for example, pop-up dialogs, e-mails) or reports published on a website (or Intranet) or printed on paper. All the pilot authorities acknowledged that this was an area that required further development.

Conclusion

The information gathered and recorded as part of the Integrated Children's System is likely to evolve over time as are the information output requirements. Some pilot authorities have ensured that relevant technical skills reside in-house to allow them to modify the exemplars or add additional data inputs and create or modify reports or other outputs produced by their IT systems. Others rely on software houses to keep their product current and in line with the changing best practice guidelines. Whichever route is taken, it is clear that IT systems developed to support the Integrated Children's System need to be adaptable to change, and to offer a range of output facilities that can support best practice. Some of the work of the pilot authorities has already been taken up and developed further by other authorities seeking to ensure that the IT systems supporting the Integrated Children's System are sufficient to meet their needs. As greater attention is given to improving the capacity of systems to retrieve the data they store, it should be possible to make more effective use of information in children's services.

Summary points
The situation prior to implementation

- All four pilot authorities had high speed networks, although these did not always extend to all users.
- Practically every practitioner polled reported having access to a computer when required. However, the use of the computer was related to the culture within the team or service, attitudes and skills of the individual and work pressures and patterns.
- Electronic information systems usually consisted of a client index database and some means of managing the processes of contact,

referral and case allocation. The recording templates for assessments and reviews were not fully integrated into the database. Social workers tended to use the system as a deposit for information rather than a source.

Developing IT to support the Integrated Children's System

- The experience of the pilot authorities suggests IT systems should:
  - be capable of dealing fully with large volumes of text data
  - include search functions for different data items and text strings
  - provide screen and report formats, for entering, viewing and printing information
  - include reports which summarise information (textual and numeric) within a child's record (such as a chronology) and across a group of children (e.g. siblings)
  - enable users to readily define filters to view or print specified sub-sets of records
  - have a user-interface which follows closely the working processes used by practitioners and enables them to easily navigate the system.
- At the time of the research none of the IT systems allowed documents received from other agencies to be scanned into the child's electronic file. The location of paper records had to be clearly noted on the child's electronic file.
- The IT systems developed to support the Integrated Children's System all incorporated workflow management – a system to guide practitioners through the key practice processes. Effective systems depended on clear business processes, sufficient flexibility to enable practitioners to respond to the complexity of day-to-day practice, and the capacity for modification to keep it up to date.
- At the time of the research the outputs from the IT systems were limited. For example, although case details could be viewed on screen, the facility for practitioners to select, draw together and print off case details was not fully developed.
- All the IT systems provided the means of recording and printing case notes, but the facility to relate them to other records held in the system, such as the chronology or core assessment, had not been fully developed.

- All the IT systems had some form of automatic notification to help safeguard and promote the welfare of children.

- The chronology was the most complex component to develop. This was due to it being dependent on information held in other exemplars, and consequently the last part of the system to be brought in. A further complication was that chronologies needed to be more than an undifferentiated list of activities. A key feature will be the capacity for practitioners to create chronologies for different audiences such as child protection case conferences, reviews and courts.

- All the IT systems could output some basic information to support the supervisory role of team managers. However, management information facilities for producing basic statistics of activity and outcome data were not fully developed.

- To ensure the validity of performance measurements, all the pilot authorities had put arrangements in place to ensure data quality.

- No IT system was fully integrated with data systems in other agencies, although some progress was being made. For example, one authority had established customised read-only screens for some schools.

- Each pilot authority had arrangements for continued upgrades and developments of their IT systems to support the Integrated Children's System.

Chapter 8

Conclusions and Implications for Policy and Practice

Background

The Integrated Children's System was designed to ensure that assessment, planning and decision making led to good outcomes for children in need and their families. It is part of the UK Government's major reform programmes for children's services in England and Wales. The System builds on earlier developments such as the Looking After Children materials and the Framework for the Assessment of Children in Need and their Families, as well as addressing current policy concerns. It is comprised of three elements:

- a framework for assessment, planning, intervention and reviewing, providing a single and coherent approach to undertaking these key processes of working with children in need

- a set of data requirements for children's services in relation to children in need and their families; these data contribute both to individual case planning and to the overall information required to plan and deliver children's services

- exemplars of case records for use by children's services practitioners to assist local authorities in developing their e-social care records for children and the IT system to support the implementation of the Integrated Children's System.

The research aimed to explore the extent to which the Integrated Children's System provides the foundation for achieving better outcomes for children. To do this the study identifies how the system impacts on: direct work with children and families; inter-agency working and information sharing; individual and strategic planning; performance management; and IT systems.

The research was carried out over two and a half years and involved four local authorities. Funding was provided by the Treasury from its Evidence Based Policy Fund in collaboration with the Department for Education and Skills and the Welsh Assembly Government. An inter-university team from England and Wales under the leadership of Royal Holloway, University of London, was commissioned to undertake the study.

To assess the impact of the Integrated Children's System base-line data was gathered using a range of methods, including: an audit of social work case files; a scrutiny of blank recording formats used by agencies other than children's social care; and interviews and questionnaire surveys with service providers from all the participating agencies. Follow-up information was gained using similar methods, including: a second audit of social work case files; multi-agency workshops; and questionnaires completed by staff in children's social care, partner agencies, and looked after young people. Questionnaires and field trips explored the IT used by local authorities to support the implementation of the Integrated Children's System.

Local authorities were supported by the research team in implementing the Integrated Children's System through training and familiarisation days, one-day conferences and the provision of a Training and Resource Pack.

Implementing the Integrated Children's System

The Integrated Children's System has a major impact on local authorities' core business because it involves a change in the way practitioners and managers in children's social care (in Wales children's social services) record, organise and use information in relation to individuals and groups of children.

A project management approach

The pilot authorities adopted a project management approach to implementation including an inter-agency group, a project group, an identified lead person, a written project plan and an issues log.

A range of strategies were used to inform and involve staff within children's social care such as focus groups, briefing papers, visits to teams and the establishment of user groups.

To involve partner agencies, authorities used existing strategic inter-agency groups. Additional support was provided through inter-agency training, and agency-specific champions and subgroups. However, because the early stages of implementation focused on achieving the necessary changes within children's social care, gaining the commitment and involvement of partner agencies was difficult. Once systems were established and limited information sharing became possible, partner agencies became more eager to be involved.

To implement the Integrated Children's System within children's social care the authorities established project groups, whose membership included representatives of practice, business/administration and IT. Their responsibility included auditing practice and business processes, IT provision and staff skills, and social work practice.

PRACTICE AND BUSINESS PROCESSES

The audit of practice and business processes gave local authorities the opportunity to examine them before incorporating them into their Integrated Children's System IT systems. For example, processes mapping resulted in some existing systems being removed while others were brought into line with current policy and best practice guidance.

IT PROVISION

The audit of IT involved three processes: an exploration of current IT systems to identify the extent of the changes and the required financial and technical resources; an audit of current IT provision to identify what additional software and hardware was needed; and an audit of staff IT skills to determine training needs and identify potential champions.

To develop current IT systems to support the Integrated Children's System one authority used their in-house IT resources, two entered into partnerships with external IT providers, and one commissioned an IT consultant. Local authorities that used external software houses, that supplied IT solutions to a number of different authorities, were often frustrated as their requests for assistance were not always prioritised. In-house IT solutions resulted in a greater degree of satisfaction because technical issues were resolved more quickly. However, this was not a low cost option as additional resources had to be brought in. When working with external providers, clear and specific contracts based on legal advice were essential.

All the pilot authorities experienced delays in fully implementing their systems. The timescale of the study meant systems had to be built quickly and sufficient time was not available to test them thoroughly; as a result local authorities experienced a range of technical issues.

SOCIAL WORK PRACTICE

A limited audit of social work case files enabled local authorities to explore the extent to which regulations and guidance were being followed and identify any existing gaps in practice skills. Three main areas of weakness were identified relating to recording, analysis, and developing plans with specific outcomes. This information was used to inform local authorities' training programmes.

For training to be effective it needed to address the background to and principles underpinning the Integrated Children's System, the required changes to practice, and the newly introduced IT system. The scale of the training was a challenge and in addition to formal training programmes other initiatives such as help-lines and practice manuals as well as cascading knowledge through team 'champions' were initiated. In addition, extensive support was given to help staff through technical glitches as they became increasingly dependent on information technology. Well-trained and confident team managers helped teams develop the necessary skills.

Continuing development

Authorities reported that implementing the Integrated Children's System incurred costs in relation to the development of and purchase of IT systems, releasing staff for training and supporting the process of implementation, costs that continued after implementation.

All the pilot authorities stressed the need to monitor the quality of the data at the point when information is initially entered. Front-line managers and administrative staff played an important role in monitoring and quality assurance.

Impact of the Integrated Children's System on recording social work practice

Local authorities' strategy and timing of implementation affects practice. During the early stages of introducing a new system, when practitioners have to learn new processes, practice temporarily deteriorates. However, once implementation was complete, the pilot authorities identified a number of positive changes to practice; and although a causal relationship is likely, it cannot be proven.

Children with complex needs

The Integrated Children's System introduces few changes to the Referral and Information Record. As a result the high rate for recording basic information about the child remained unchanged. However, in areas where recording was poor, for example parental awareness of a referral and the outcome of referrals, it led to substantial improvements.

The main change to the assessments of children in need who are living at home is the greater emphasis on planning. For example, prior to the Integrated Children's System initial assessments were not linked to formal plans; a plan now follows the initial assessment. The findings suggest that most initial assessments that result in further action by children's social care now result in a formal plan.

The fundamental change to the core assessment was to separate the child's plan from the assessment record. This has resulted in significantly more detailed information being recorded, although the quality of recording, particularly in relation to parenting capacity and wider family and environmental factors, needs greater attention.

Children in need of protection

Prior to the Integrated Children's System there was no specific format to systematically record key child protection processes. New records for children in need of protection were introduced. The findings suggest that social work recording on the new Record of Strategy Discussion and the Record of Outcome of s47 Enquiries is of a notably high standard.

The Integrated Children's System has had a positive impact on recording Initial Child Protection Conference Reports; of particular significance is the improvement to the quality of the analysis. However, the impact on Child Protection Reviews has been more mixed. Although the quantity and quality for recording children's developmental needs, parenting capacity and family and environmental factors increased significantly, the rate of recording the summary of the review discussion and the reason for the decision decreased.

Children looked after

The Integrated Children's System introduces the greatest change for practitioners working with looked after children. To ensure that historical information is linked to a child's current circumstances the Essential Information Record Part 2 is replaced by a Chronology. The change has had a varied effect on recording; while some areas show a substantial increase, others have decreased. The findings suggest two factors affect the Chronology: confusion over its purpose (practitioners generally see it as tool to gather key information while IT experts regard it as an output of what is held on the data base) and difficulties over its layout and content (courts require a different format and additional information). Work, to resolve these problems, is being taken forward by the Department for Children, Schools and Families.

The Integrated Children's System replaces the Placement Plan with the Placement Information Record. This record is completed at the time a child becomes looked after and contains key information for carers. The change has had little impact on recording practice. For example, recording the reasons and type of placement remains high, while recording children's emotional and behavioural development continues to be poor, information key to carers' understanding of the child.

A key change introduced by the Integrated Children's System is that all children entering the care system should have an up-to-date core assessment. The findings show that this is beginning to change practice; a core assessment was found in half the cases. However, the Integrated Children's System has made little impact on the endemic failure to routinely monitor the progress of children looked after over time, and, although completed Assessment and Progress Records were not expected on case files, no records (regardless of their stage of completion) were found on the case files post implementation.

The new Care Plan is in two parts. Part 1 covers the assessment of the child's needs and applies to all children looked after, while Part 2 identifies the services and actions needed to respond to these needs. When appropriate the Adoption Plan or the Pathway Plan replaces Part 2 of the Care Plan. The Care Plan covers the birth parent and corporate parenting (corporate parenting refers to the local authority including those responsible for the day-to-day care of the child).

The findings suggest that the changes to the Care Plan have either had little impact on recording or brought about improvements. For example, some aspects were unaffected such as recording the legal status of the child, the reason for care and the chosen Care Plan which remained high. Of particular interest is the significant improvement in relation to the quality of recording children's developmental needs and the strategies to meet them.

In general the implementation of the Integrated Children's System improved the recording of the Pathway Plan. Aspects of recording which were good prior to implementation remained unchanged. Real improvements were found in relation to recording information on the young person's family and social relationships and their emotional and behavioural development; these were now found in practically every case. Moreover, the quality of much of the recording improved significantly.

The Integrated Children's System has not significantly affected the information recorded on Reviews for children looked after in relation to their developmental needs. The main change is the introduction of birth parents and corporate parents into the review process. The impact of this is similar to that found for Care Plans; information relating to birth parents is more likely to be included in the review than corporate parenting.

The impact on recording – social workers' perceptions

The Integrated Children's System impacted on all aspects of recording social work practice and a key element to its success would be the training and support provided by local authorities. At the time of the study approximately half the practitioners reported having attended training on the Integrated Children's System. The lack of training was reflected in the views they expressed; many reported that insufficient training was hindering their understanding of the system and their ability to use it effectively.

Impact on recording practice

The impact of the Integrated Children's System on social work practice is significant; over three-quarters of social workers reported that their practice had changed. Most social workers and managers also reported changes in the reports and assessments received from colleagues within their own organisation; some changes were welcomed (greater focus and less narrative), others were not (unnecessary paperwork).

Changes related to both the amount and quality of the information recorded. Increases in the amount of information reflected both positive outcomes, such as focusing on individual children rather than sibling groups, and negative outcomes, such as some IT systems not allowing information to populate from one record to another. The impact of the Integrated Children's

System had a mixed effect on the quality of recording. A similar proportion of practitioners thought quality had improved as thought it had deteriorated, although the largest group felt that little had changed. Positive changes related to more focused assessments and clearer plans.

A substantial proportion of social work practitioners thought the Integrated Children's System formats were not family friendly and would have an adverse impact on direct practice. This suggests confusion over their purpose; they were not designed as tools to carry out direct work with children and families. For example, social workers raised concerns over the language and terminology used in the exemplars, their size and the change from family to child focused reports which resulted in much duplication for some families. Although children have a right to access their records, specific reports may need to be written to take account of the communication skills and the sensitivities of families. The timescale of the research meant that there had been little time for local authorities to review the way they output information for children and families.

Impact on the use of IT

The Integrated Children's System increases the amount of time social work practitioners spent using IT and changes the way IT is used, away from word processing and email towards data entry and retrieval. Although the change from hand written to electronic recording will increase the time spent using IT, the findings suggest that practitioners' resentment to the change owes much to unresolved problems with IT systems and their unfamiliarity with new systems.

Practically three-quarters of social work practitioners received IT training following the introduction of the Integrated Children's System in their authority. Training focused on data entry tasks, reflecting the changing role IT played in social work practice. One-off courses cannot meet the changing and developing skills of practitioners. Additional support was provided through telephone helplines, experts or super-users, administrators and technicians.

Impact of the Integrated Children's System on inter-agency working

If information is to be shared it is essential that it is recorded in a manner that accurately identifies the child, uses a common language, and stores the information in a manner that supports electronic exchange.

The findings show that the formats used by health, education, youth justice and police all record personal information about the child to ensure an accurate identification. However, the language used differs considerably as did the range of information recorded.

All practitioners who work with children and families need to understand how the Integrated Children's System affects their practice. The findings suggest the process of informing practitioners working with children has started. Of the 131 professionals (from health, children's social care, education, youth justice and the police) questioned, half reported having attended a multi-agency briefing session.

In exploring how the Integrated Children's System affected inter-agency working the study focused on the information requested from agencies, assessments and reports completed by agencies, information received by agencies, electronic information exchange, and inter-agency practice.

Information requested from agencies

The Integrated Children's System affected the type of information requested by agencies working with children. Changes generally related to the type of information rather than to any increase in the amount or quality of information. The agencies most likely to request different information were children's social care, education and health.

Assessments and reports

There is some evidence to suggest that agencies, such as health and education, are beginning to use the conceptual framework of the Integrated Children's System to structure parts of their reports which are to be shared with children's social care.

Information received by agencies

The Integrated Children's System affected the reports and assessments received by agencies working with children. Professionals in health and education reported changes to the documentation they received from children's social care. The changes had a mixed reception; practitioners welcomed the improvements in the quality of information but resented any duplication.

Electronic information exchange

The Integrated Children's System has started to impact on the amount of information exchanged electronically between agencies working with children. The extent to which this had progressed within an authority reflects the stage of its implementation process. Once systems are firmly embedded in children's social care, authorities turned their attention to developing initiatives to exchange information electronically.

Inter-agency practice

The impact of the Integrated Children's System on inter-agency practice was explored through asking practitioners to comment on four issues: policy and practice; information sharing; clarification of roles and responsibilities; and quality of inter-agency working.

The findings show that, regardless of which of these four issues were under consideration, most professionals thought relatively little had changed in regard to inter-agency activities as a result of the Integrated Children's System. When change was reported, in the majority of cases professionals stated things had improved. The increase in inter-agency collaboration was greatest between health, education and children's social care and to a lesser degree between these agencies and the police and youth offending teams. The findings suggest improved inter-agency collaboration was dependent on an existing culture of inter-agency working, the authority's approach to implementation, and how long the system had been in place.

Impact of the Integrated Children's System on involving children and young people

The examination of social work files suggests social workers are more conscientious in recording the participation and involvement of some groups of children and young people than others.

Recording the views of children and young people

Recording the views of children in need of protection is still not common place, although it has improved (noted in 14 per cent of cases post implementation). Traditionally, children looked after are more likely to be involved in plans and decisions that affect them, but the findings suggest the Integrated Children's System has yet to have a positive impact. In contrast, the implementation of the Integrated Children's System has substantially improved the extent to which young people are involved in Pathway Plans and the recording of this information.

Young people's experiences

A group of 34 young people looked after in one pilot authority completed questionnaires that explored their experiences of the system. Their views provide insights into the extent to which young people are involved in the process of care planning and review since the implementation of the Integrated Children's System.

All the young people thought that they should be involved in drawing up their care plan. However, a third felt they had not participated, reinforcing the findings from the scrutiny of social work case files.

The Integrated Children's System may have had some impact on the extent to which young people felt consulted on the detailed planning of their review meetings. Comparisons with the findings from earlier research suggest that, although consultation in relation to venue and timing has changed little, deciding who should be invited was more likely to be done in conjunction with young people.

Young people were generally content with the degree of professional involvement in their care plans and reviews, but they wanted parents and family members to play a greater role. However, the findings suggest that, although parental attendance is less than young people would wish, it has improved.

Young people held decided opinions on the issues that should be included in care plans and reviews. The majority thought plans and reviews should cover contact with family members, living arrangements, education, health, and family and social relationships, but more sensitive issues such as the young person's past, their friends and feelings were not always seen as appropriate subjects for discussion in such a forum.

The findings suggest that young people's experience of reviews had improved. The majority of those involved in the study reported having received some written information explaining the purpose of their forthcoming review, and when at the review feeling able to voice their views or dissent; in most cases issues were resolved satisfactorily. Moreover, approximately two-thirds of young people recalled that their reviews had led to a decision and knew who was responsible for carrying it out. In practically every case the young person understood the reason for the decision and most agreed with it.

However, despite the greater specificity of decisions not all young people were confident that they would be implemented; indeed a fifth were very cynical.

Young people need to know the outcome of their reviews; approximately half had been provided a copy of the report. Simply providing a copy of the review is not always appropriate and young people expressed a wish for something shorter and more accessible.

Use of information technology

It is important to make the distinction between the Integrated Children's System and the IT systems that support it. The Integrated Children's System is not an IT system in itself, but the volume and complexity of the information it requires means that it needs to be underpinned by appropriate information technology. The range and type of outputs required to support practice at all levels of the organisation form a significant element to be considered in developing IT systems to underpin the Integrated Children's System.

Implementation of the Integrated Children's System requires close collaboration between IT staff and practitioners; it is unlikely to succeed where it is regarded as the exclusive responsibility of either group.

The pilot showed that implementation of the Integrated Children's System required local authorities to address wider issues in the development of their IT systems. Single data entry, text handling, data cloning and information sharing between agencies were all raised as important questions to be resolved. It also highlighted the need to improve the provision of hardware as well as the functionality of the system.

The authorities differed substantially in how information was entered into their IT system, and in particular the use of administrative staff. The relationship between the roles of administrative staff and practitioners in their use of IT was a key issue throughout.

Specifically, the evaluation showed that, by the end of the pilot:

- there were still issues in relation to practitioner access to computers in some authorities

- some teams still had difficulty in accessing the IT system; of particular concern was the fact that, in two authorities, emergency duty teams still did not have network access, substantially compromising their ability to retrieve electronic files outside office hours

- all authorities had introduced automatic warnings or flags to indicate special needs or risks; all had introduced alerts to indicate that assessments and reviews were due (or were in the process of doing so); all but one authority had automatic notification if a case record had been changed by another user

- none of the pilot authorities had yet been able to provide practitioners with the facility to select and print off case summary details using items drawn from different exemplars; developing a flexible IT system to support the Integrated Children's System was considered a key element in successful implementation

- none of the pilot authorities had a fully implemented chronology facility that could collate different types of event into a single sequence

- the process for enabling practitioners and managers to produce simple customised statistical reports without being reliant on IT staff, such as lists of those children whose outcomes fell outside a performance target, or reports of all children due to sit Standard Assessment Tests (SATs), was receiving considerable attention but needed further development in all authorities; such a facility was considered essential in developing the Integrated Children's System as a tool to support performance management at practitioner, team and strategic levels

- IT systems in all four authorities included the facility for team and other managers to see a list of children assigned to the team, with unallocated cases identified; three authorities had the facility to produce cross-views for foster placements and carers, though in one access was limited to administrative staff.

In addition, the evaluation revealed that further attention needed to be given to system security and the recording of structured data on services provided by agencies outside social care. Of key importance was a further finding that electronic case management records were not yet routinely reviewed during supervision meetings. The development of such a practice is regarded as fundamental to successful implementation.

Authorities were beginning to consider how they might add multi-agency facilities to the IT systems supporting the Integrated Children's System: while none were fully integrated with the systems available to other agencies, two authorities had established one-way information flows with education and one was in the process of developing these for health, housing and the police.

It is likely that implementation of the Integrated Children's System acts as a catalyst for improving the overall functionality of information systems in children's social care.

The general conclusion of three of the four pilot authorities was that, by the end of the study, their IT systems were meeting the Integrated Children's System requirements relatively well, though not entirely meeting the needs of practitioners.

Implications for policy and practice
Implementation
FLEXIBLE SYSTEMS

The Integrated Children's System has been designed to ensure that assessment, planning and decision making lead to good outcomes for children in need and their families. Implementation of the Integrated Children's System should not stop with its introduction. For the system to continue to be relevant and effective it must be sufficiently flexible to accommodate changes in legislation, government regulations and guidance, and practice. The findings suggest that it is important to ensure arrangements are established to obtain feedback from practitioners and managers using the system and to respond to their comments.

IT systems to support the Integrated Children's System can be developed in a variety of ways and the findings from the research suggest they all have advantages and disadvantages. Successful partnerships between local authorities and external providers are supported through:

- drawing up clear and specific contracts based on legal advice
- ensuring the IT system includes all relevant practice and business processes, has the ability to be modified, and is able to produce a range of outputs that support both practitioners and managers in their tasks; these will include alerts reminders, summary reports, cross-views and statistical tables.

MANAGING THE PROCESS

Implementing the Integrated Children's System will involve local authorities in major changes because it affects the way children's social care carries out its core business. The experience of the pilot authorities suggests adopting a planned project management approach to implementation, which includes a strategic inter-agency steering group, an implementation group within children's social care, an identified lead person, a written project plan and an issues log, is particularly successful.

The implementation groups were primarily responsible for a range of issues fundamental to the successful introduction of the Integrated Children's System within children's social care. To be successful the implementation group should have defined roles and responsibilities and be provided with the necessary resources to do the job.

Local authorities need to have a comprehensive understanding of what changes are needed and how to best deploy their limited resources. Because the Integrated Children's System affects all aspects of the work of children's social care, local authorities should audit their existing practice and business processes, IT provision and staff skills, and social work practice.

The Integrated Children's System is not a solution to existing practice problems and it will initially highlight shortcomings and difficulties. The findings suggest that training on practice issues in advance of implementation, particularly in relation to recording, assessment and analysis, can help practitioners when the system is introduced. Training programmes should be iterative and address the challenges and issues that arise at different points in the implementation process.

All agencies working with children and young people need to understand the relevance of the system to them, and how it will benefit the children and young people with whom they work. Inter-agency implementation groups which involve representatives with sufficient seniority from all relevant agencies have proved to be a successful model for driving forward the Integrated Children's System.

SUPPORT FOR SOCIAL WORK PRACTITIONERS

For implementation to be successful all staff within children's social care need to understand the reason for change and how it will benefit the children and families they work with. Front-line managers and champions are essential to successful implementation and sustained change. In order to undertake their responsibilities managers and identified champions need to be provided with the necessary training and resources to support their teams and colleagues.

REALISTIC EXPECTATIONS

The Integrated Children's System requires practitioners to use new processes and systems. The findings suggest that during the initial stages of implementation, when IT issues are being resolved and practitioners are learning new skills, practice temporarily deteriorates. Local authorities' implementation strategy should be informed by this phenomenon and ensure staff training and support is timely and on-going. Due regard should be taken by managers and those responsible for quality assurance, audit and inspection of the fact that practice is unlikely to show immediate improvement and in fact may deteriorate. Expectations of the effectiveness of the Integrated Children's System should be realistic during the early stage of implementation.

Changing social work practice

TRAINING

The degree of change experienced by practitioners as a result of the implementation of the Integrated Children's System is not uniform across children's social care. The findings show that where the Integrated Children's System records differ little to current, well-used materials practice remains relatively stable. Newly introduced records have resulted in improved practice but where significant changes to well-established systems are introduced the impact is varied. The challenge local authorities face is to engender confidence in busy practitioners who are comfortable with existing systems that devoting time and energy to learning new ways of working and recording will have real benefits for the children and families they work with. Support and training should be targeted at those teams that are experiencing the greatest degree of change.

Line managers in teams experiencing the greatest level of change have a crucial role to play in supporting their practitioners. Training should be targeted at line managers to ensure they understand the changes to practice and have the required skills to use the electronic recording system confidently. It is the responsibility of line managers to monitor recording practice, use supervision to identify gaps in practitioners' knowledge, and conduct internal quality assurance exercises. The resulting information should inform the authority's training programme and where necessary to commission additional support and help.

MONITORING PRACTICE

The findings suggest that the Integrated Children's System has generally had a positive impact on practice and recording involving children in need who are living in the community. However, its impact on work with children looked after is more varied. Of particular concern is the continuing failure to monitor routinely their long term progress. It is the responsibility of line managers to ensure practitioners regularly assess the development and progress of children placed in long-term care and that the information from these assessments is linked to the current robust system for reviewing the needs and care plans for looked after children.

The Integrated Children's System has had a positive impact on Pathway Plans, and the relationship between assessment and planning has become more explicit. However, a lack of contingency planning was a feature in social work records both before and after implementation. Moving to independence is a time of considerable change and adjustment for young people and even the best laid plans frequently do not work out as intended. Managers and practitioners responsible for developing Pathway Plans with young people will need to devote greater resources to ensuring alternative options and ideas are explored to inform the contingency plans.

Promoting inter-agency working

AGREED LANGUAGE

All agencies working with children record basic information about individuals; however, the terminology varied considerably. An agreed language and format should be developed that accurately identifies the child and his or her needs and enables, when required, information to be shared electronically.

PROTOCOLS AND PROCEDURES

Practitioners from different agencies and organisations were anxious how the Data Protection Act 1998 impacts on their ability to share information, and in resolving uncertainty they are overly dependent on personal contacts. Agencies and organisations who work with children and families should develop agreed joint protocols, procedures and guidelines for information sharing that guide practitioners in making professional judgements about what to share, in what circumstances, and for what purposes. These should be in line with Government Guidance on information sharing which is readily available to practitioners in all agencies working with children (HM Goverment 2006d).

Different working cultures and priorities between adult and children's services hamper information sharing. All organisations and agencies need to ensure that their staff are aware that section 11 of the Children Act 2004 and

Government Guidance (HM Government 2006e) make it clear that adult services have a duty to take account of safeguarding and promoting the welfare of children when exercising their normal functions.

CHANNELS OF COMMUNICATION

Effective information sharing and collaborative working can be hampered by many issues. To ensure these are minimised organisations and agencies working with children and families will need to establish effective channels of communication. However, professional confidence in information sharing will not improve unless agencies invest the necessary resources to ensure colleagues in other agencies are kept up to date with key decisions and developments in the cases in which they are jointly involved.

THRESHOLDS FOR SERVICES

All agencies and organisations working with children and families should ensure greater clarity over the thresholds for their services. The introduction of the Common Assessment Framework will necessitate these agencies working more closely together, a process which should promote greater understanding of one another. In addition, agencies represented on the Local Safeguarding Children Board should ensure the Board fulfils its function in setting thresholds for intervention when there are concerns about a child's safety.

INTER-AGENCY TRAINING

Practitioners from all the agencies identified a lack of training as a major factor in limiting the potential of the Integrated Children's System. Local Safeguarding Children Boards should identify the training needs arising from the Integrated Children's System and use this information to inform their planning and commissioning of training. Training on the Integrated Children's System should ensure all agencies and organisations become familiar with the system and understand their expected contribution to assessment, analysis and review of children in need.

INTER-AGENCY PRACTICE

The findings suggest that the Integrated Children's System is beginning to have a positive impact on inter-agency practice. Initiatives for information sharing were more successful when they built on existing procedures, were strongly led, and had the full commitment of senior management within children's social care and other key agencies working with children.

CHILDREN'S SOCIAL CARE

For staff working in children's social care, the implementation of the Integrated Children's System introduces new electronic methods for recording information and resulted in changes to both the amount and quality of the recorded information. Children's social care need to ensure that changes to the amount of information reflect improvements in practice rather than inadequate IT systems that require practitioners to continually re-enter the same data.

A substantial number of practitioners felt the formality and length of the exemplars negatively impacted on their ability to work with families. Because the exemplars were developed primarily to record the core processes of social work practice (and not intended as an aid to direct practice) they are not particularly family friendly. Children's social care should work to develop outputs that can more appropriately be shared with children and families. IT systems are primarily tools to support practitioners and managers; social workers will need support to produce specific reports for children and families which take account of their communication needs and sensitivities.

USE OF IT WITHIN CHILDREN'S SOCIAL CARE

The Integrated Children's System has changed the way practitioners use IT, shifting from simply using it to carry out administrative functions towards accessing and aggregating data in order to manage work better. Children's social care will need to ensure that IT training provides practitioners and managers with the necessary skills on data entry, retrieval and data aggregation so that they can confidently take full advantage of their system. An audit of existing IT skills will ensure that training courses are designed to take account of the differing levels of confidence and skills that exist within the practitioner group.

Although the increased training on the systems to support the Integrated Children's System is essential, care must be taken that fundamental aspects of IT are not forgotten. Training which covers 'core' skills will always be necessary if practitioners are to feel in control of their IT systems and not merely data entry workers. In addition, these 'core' skills will seed benefits to practitioners which are directly related to the Integrated Children's System both in terms of their IT usage in general, and their continued professional development.

Local authorities will need to anticipate the changing needs of their practitioners and ensure training courses and other forms of support are sufficiently flexible. In addition to formal training courses authorities should consider introducing telephone help-lines, technical support and experts or super-users.

Involving children and young people in assessments and reviews

MONITORING RECORDING

Recording the involvement of, and consultation with, children and young people is crucial to understanding the degree to which they participate in assessments, plans and reviews. The findings suggest this is not always being done. The Integrated Children's System should make monitoring recording practice easier; line managers need to be more robust in carrying out this duty.

CONSULTING CHILDREN AND YOUNG PEOPLE

The Integrated Children's System has yet to impact on the involvement of children in need, who live at home, in their assessments and reviews. For example, the scrutiny of records suggests children are not routinely consulted during initial assessments, child protection conferences or in the planning process. Managers need to ensure that whenever possible all children and young people are involved and greater use made of available resources and toolkits to enable young children and those with disabilities to express their views and fully participate.

Although children and young people looked after are more likely than children living at home to be consulted during assessments, care planning and reviews, nonetheless less than half participate. The level of consultation has changed little with the implementation of the Integrated Children's System. Formats for consulting children and young people were introduced with the Looking After Children materials. The Integrated Children's System did not introduce new ones, assuming that this would result in duplication and confusion. Managers should make sure children and young people looked after are consulted and fully involved, and that formats to support this process are readily available and used.

Young people's involvement in their Pathway Plans has improved with the implementation of the Integrated Children's System; nonetheless, some

30 per cent of young people are not consulted. Managers should ensure that all young people are consulted and fully involved in their Pathway Plans. A failure to do so may result in unrealistic plans that are unlikely to be met, or in plans that are not in line with young people's wishes and are subsequently rejected.

PROVIDING YOUNG PEOPLE WITH KEY DOCUMENTS

The reports of young people looked after in one pilot authority suggest that they were not routinely provided with copies of plans or reviews. Managers and practitioners should ensure that young people looked after are given a record of their care plan and review in a format that takes account of their level of understanding and method of communication. Providing copies of plans and reports is not enough; care plans and review reports should be discussed with young people.

PARENTAL INVOLVEMENT IN PLANS AND REVIEWS

Most young people in the one participating local authority were satisfied with the involvement of professionals in their care plans, but although the majority wanted birth parents to participate this rarely happened. Managers should ensure that parents receive the support they need to continue (where appropriate) to play a role in the lives of their children once they become looked after.

INCREASING YOUNG PEOPLE'S PARTICIPATION

The reports of young people suggest consulting them about their reviews has shown some improvement; nonetheless approximately half of those questioned felt excluded. The ability to participate fully depends on careful preparation and ongoing support during the review. Managers need to support practitioners to ensure young people are involved in the planning process and are adequately prepared.

Most young people were aware of the decisions made as a result of review meetings, but were cynical over the extent to which they would come to fruition. Review Chairs will need to ensure decisions are carried out or that children and young people understand the reasons which have prevented them.

Developing IT systems

Findings from the pilot include important messages for both policymakers and senior managers in local authorities concerning the development of IT systems to support the implementation and successful use of the Integrated Children's System.

IT ISSUES FOR POLICYMAKERS

Policymakers need to be aware that implementation of the Integrated Children's System as an electronic case-management system is a lengthy process. All the pilot authorities found their implementation plans were over-optimistic both in terms of time and resources required to produce a fully operational IT system that adequately supported the implementation of the Integrated Children's System. They also found implementation to be both demanding and difficult, for it forced them to confront longstanding issues that were not directly part of the Integrated Children's System but rather concerned the wider use of information which had yet to be resolved. There were many obstacles to be overcome before the gains became apparent.

The pilot also revealed that any subsequent programme to improve the Integrated Children's System will need to address the finding that the system does not currently encourage the recording of essential details concerning children and their families if these are not captured at referral or initial assessment. There is currently no clear process step for amending or completing these details if new facts emerge at a later stage. The result is that important fields are often left blank, a factor that will negatively impact on the ability for practitioners to produce useful chronologies.

IT ISSUES FOR AUTHORITIES

Successful implementation of the Integrated Children's System as an electronic case-recording system requires: dedicated funding; a project management team with time set aside for the task; staff with IT skills and knowledge included on the project management team; and contingency plans to cover technological problems. Preparations and planning for implementation are important factors. These ideally include an audit of hardware, software and IT skills. Free communication between users of the system and software developers is essential to successful implementation. Including users from all levels of the authority in this dialogue can be very valuable.

It is important to note that implementation is an iterative process, with IT requirements constantly emerging as the potential of the Integrated Children's System becomes apparent. Authorities will need to ensure that their systems are sufficiently flexible to take account of continuing requests from users as well as modifications to meet new government requirements.

Authorities will need to consider how their system can be developed in such a way as to produce outputs that support both practitioners and managers in their tasks. These will include reminders, summary reports and statistical tables. Facilities to allow users to select data items to be included in reports will be an important element in successful use of the system. Developing a flexible system that can respond to new requests is the key message.

As part of the implementation plan, authorities will need to explore how their administrative staff can best support practitioners in implementing and using the Integrated Children's System. There were considerable differences between the pilot authorities concerning how this issue was addressed, and there are important messages to be learnt from their experience.

Finally, it is evident that successful implementation will depend on how far the capacity of the system is exploited. Successful implementation will have been achieved when the system is set up to produce automatic alerts, reminders and data transfers, when managers become accustomed to select data and analyse reports without recourse to technicians, and when it becomes routine to use the electronic system and its facilities as a basis for supervision.

Aims and Methods

Aims of the study

The present study was funded for two and a half years to provide information which could be used to develop further and refine the Integrated Children's System in preparation for implementation in 2006. As was outlined in the introductory chapter, the commissioners comprised a cross-government group including the Evidence Based Policy Fund, the Department of Health (continued by the Department for Education and Skills, now the Department for Children, Schools and Families), the Welsh Assembly Government, the Connexions service, and the Children and Young People's Unit.

The research study through pilots in England and Wales aimed to explore whether the Integrated Children's System:

- improves the quality of direct work with children and families
- provides the foundation for achieving better outcomes for children
- supports inter-agency working and facilitates information sharing
- provides the information needed to support planning processes at both individual and strategic levels
- assists the use and development of performance management.

Another set of aims related to the authorities' IT systems developed to support the Integrated Children's System. These aims explored:

- the extent to which the Integrated Children's System IT implementation impacts on a pilot authority's overall IT plans
- how well the functionality of the IT systems met operational needs
- the advantages and disadvantages in the different approaches taken by authorities in the development and implementation of their Integrated Children's System IT systems.

The study was carried out with the support and guidance of both a research advisory group and a development group.

The Research Advisory Group

The Research Advisory Group had two purposes: first, to keep informed the many interests across government in England and Wales about the progress of the study, and second, to inform and seek advice from key research academics and stakeholders while the study was running.

Membership of the group was as inclusive as possible and comprised representatives from: relevant government departments and the Welsh Assembly Government, managers and practitioners from the participating local authorities, specialist services for children, relevant voluntary bodies and user groups, relevant academics and members of the research team.

Progress reports were submitted to the Advisory Group throughout the study. The Advisory Group met on three occasions and provided valuable support and guidance.

The Development Group

The purpose of the Development Group was to ensure an ongoing exchange of information between policy makers and the research team. This was a key aspect of the study because the Integrated Children's System was being piloted at a time of much policy development and change, for example during the timeframe of the research the Children Act 2004 was being debated and refined, and government guidance for 'Working Together to Safeguard Children' was being revised (see the introductory chapter for more details). It was, therefore, essential that early findings from the study informed government decision making and, in turn, that members of the research team were kept up to date with all relevant policy changes. The Development Group consisted of representatives from the then Department for Education and Skills (now the Department for Children, Schools and Families), the Welsh Assembly Government, the Council for Disabled Children, the Race Equality Unit, members of a parallel government funded study of the Integrated Children's System (York University), and the research team.

To support local authorities in preparing for implementing the Integrated Children's System the Department of Health and the Welsh Assembly Government (2002) organised a number of initiatives to ensure changes and developments in government policy and emerging findings from the research were made widely available. These included a series of briefing papers on the Integrated Children's System initiated prior to the start of the research. The Development Group provided guidance on how the findings from the study should inform Briefing Papers 6, 7 and 8 which were produced during the course of the research (Department of Health and Department for Education and Skills 2000–2005).

In addition, the Department for Education and Skills held a series of regional conferences to enable local authorities to keep abreast of relevant policy changes, the emerging findings from the research and the experiences of the pilot authorities when preparing for implementing the Integrated Children's System. The Development Group provided the forum at which the design and content of each conference was discussed.

Research governance

The research project was subject to the Royal Holloway, University of London, ethics approval process and adhered to the 2003 ethical guidelines laid down by the Social Research Association (www.the-sra.org.uk/ ethical.htm) and the Research Governance Framework for Health and Social Care (Department of Health 2006).

The collection of case-related data was restricted to children's social care. The Research Group of the Association of Directors of Social Services gave their approval to the study and recommended it to all local authorities. In other agencies, such as health, education and youth justice, only documentary evidence was scrutinised; no individual case data were examined. However, the views of practitioners were sought through questionnaires and interviews.

The members of the research team were either qualified social workers or child psychologists and had considerable experience in carrying out research-focused interviews. Criminal records bureau checks on members of the research team were carried out prior to any interviews taking place.

Methodology

In order to evaluate the impact of the Integrated Children's System on practice within the pilot authorities a combination of research methods was used.

> Our view is that insufficient use is made of combined methodologies in pilot evaluations, which can provide insights that are inaccessible to any single method. (Jowell 2003, p.30)

The work fell into a number of distinct stages and included:

- selecting the local authorities and establishing the study – three English and one Welsh
- gathering the baseline data
- providing training to staff on the Integrated Children's System
- local authorities implement and use the Integrated Children's System for six months
- gathering follow-up data.

Stage 1: Selecting the local authorities and establishing the study

The aim of the research was to work in partnership with four local authorities and involve social services, health, education, police and youth justice. The primary criterion for selection was contrasting patterns of co-operation and co-working between these services.

In August 2002 a letter was sent to all local authority chief executives in England and Wales from their governments, inviting them to put forward their local authority and partner agencies to pilot an integrated approach to the delivery of services to children and their families. Those interested in becoming involved were asked to submit a range of documentary evidence in support of their application.

Applications were received from 28 local authorities. Members of the research team and policy makers were responsible for short-listing nine authorities using predetermined criteria. In order to inform the final selection, a member of the research team visited each short-listed authority during November 2002. The aim of the visit was to identify:

- the level of commitment in principle from children's social care and partner agencies to pilot the Integrated Children's System
- the extent to which the Assessment Framework and the Looking After Children materials were currently being used
- the degree of collaborative working between children's social care and other agencies
- the extent to which children and families are involved
- whether their IT systems would have the capacity to implement the Integrated Children's System within the required timescale.

This was done through talking to key staff, scrutinising documentary evidence and auditing a limited number of social work case files. Anonymised reports of the nine site visits and supporting written evidence were produced and submitted to the selection panel for consideration. The members of the selection panel included policy makers and members of the research team who had not been involved in the site visits or the production of the reports. The selection of the four pilot sites was made on the basis of the information in these reports.

The four successful authorities, referred to in the report as Shire County, Welsh Local Authority, London Borough and Unitary Authority, differed in relation to type, physical size and constituency; a detailed description can be found in Chapter 2.

In December 2002 the chosen authorities were informed that their application had been successful. Following this, members of the research team met with senior managers from all the key agencies in each authority. The meetings were used to explore a number of issues, including: how best to establish the pilot within the authority, the procedures to notify families of the pilot, the timetabling of the data gathering, and the timing and content of the training programme. In addition, a link person within each service within the participating authority, who had sufficient seniority to ensure decisions were acted upon, was identified to ensure good communication between their agency and the research team.

Stage 2: Collection of baseline data

To evaluate the impact of the Integrated Children's System on social work practice, inter-agency co-operation and information sharing requirements, baseline data were collected. To gain a comprehensive picture of practice prior to the implementation of the Integrated Children's System, different methods were used to collect data. These included: a scrutiny of documentary evidence; interviews and questionnaires to key service providers; and an audit of social work case files.

The audit of case files was restricted to children's social care for two reasons. First, the Integrated Children's System reflects the processes of children's social care and has evolved from two systems developed within social services for interventions with children, young people and their families: the Assessment Framework and the Looking After Children systems. Consequently the Integrated Children's System will result in major changes to the way professionals working in children's social care record information about children and their families.

A second and more practical reason was the concern about the length of time it might take to ensure that all the appropriate consents and approvals were in place before data could be gathered from the case files of partner agencies; gaining the approval of the relevant ethical committees could result in the research being delayed by approximately 12–18 months which was beyond the timeframe of the research. Instead, the partner agencies submitted blank copies of the formats they completed regularly on children and families. These were used to identify what data are commonly collected and the language used to describe these data items.

The original intention had been to interview young people who were looked after both before and after the implementation of the Integrated Children's System with a special focus on care planning, assessment and review. However, discussions with managers in children's social care revealed that the study's timeframe meant two discrete groups would be needed because few young people would have experienced assessments or reviews under both systems. With the advice of the Research Advisory Group, it was decided to use existing research findings on looked after young people's experiences of assessments and reviews to act as a baseline. The current study only sought the views of young people after the implementation of the Integrated Children's System.

A SCRUTINY OF DOCUMENTARY EVIDENCE

A key objective of the scrutiny of documentary evidence was to develop an understanding of current practice with regard to inter-agency collaboration and information sharing. This was done through a further analysis of the protocols and procedures submitted by each authority when seeking to participate in the study. Where information was missing, additional data were sought from the relevant agency. In addition, to explore the consistencies and differences in the information routinely gathered by the partner agencies (health, education, youth offending teams and the police), blank copies of their recording formats were requested. This resulted in 169 records: 92 from health, 59 from education, 13 from youth offending teams, and 5 from the police. These included referral and/or information records, initial assessments, ongoing assessments, in-depth assessment and plans. However, no review formats were sent to the research team.

In order to exchange information effectively and work collaboratively depends on a common language and agreed definitions. Moreover, there is an expectation that information sharing within the Integrated Children's System will be electronic in the future; current differences in recording and definitions will, therefore, be brought into greater focus. The scrutiny of documentary evidence was used to identify the potential challenges that would face agencies in working to drive forward the Government's information sharing agenda.

INTERVIEWS AND QUESTIONNAIRES WITH SERVICE PROVIDERS

The original aim had been to interview a sample of five line managers and frontline staff from children's social care, health, education and youth justice in each participating local authority. This would have resulted in a sample of 20 professionals from each authority; a total of 80 interviews.

However, the number and range of professionals interviewed changed as the result of a specific request from the participating authorities. Initial meetings with the local authorities had highlighted the close working relationship between the police and social services; it was thought that the views of the police should be included. In addition, the larger local authorities felt that limiting the number of interviews to five per agency would not capture the range of services and experiences. For example, Shire County children's social care is linked with eight primary care trusts. To provide a more accurate reflection of the experiences of agencies it was agreed that each agency would be offered up to eight interviews. Finally, to enable every professional within health, education, police, youth justice and children's social care the opportunity to participate in the study, a questionnaire was developed based on the interview schedule.

The semi-structured interview conducted with professionals covered the following issues:

- their knowledge of the roles and responsibilities of other agencies in relation to vulnerable children and families
- the impact of current practice and procedures for working with other relevant agencies
- their experience of contact and co-operation between agencies working with vulnerable children and families
- their experience of joint working and information sharing between relevant agencies
- their experience of accessing data collected by other agencies but which are necessary to inform their work with vulnerable children and families

- their experience of using aggregated information about children, and their views on how the reporting functions of management information systems can be improved.

The interview schedule was piloted with colleagues from a number of agencies and amended in the light of feedback.

In order to ensure the views of a range of different personnel in each agency were included in the interview study, the nominated link person within the agency identified professionals (managers or practitioners) who represented a breadth of skills, experience and knowledge. For example, one department of children's social care nominated the following personnel:

- a team leader representing family support services
- a team leader for aftercare services
- a team leader representing the assessment team
- a practitioner from the team providing services to disabled children and young people
- a reviewing officer working with complex cases of children looked after.

The selection resulted in 85 interviews being carried out. Table A.1 shows how they were distributed between the services and across the local authorities.

The questionnaire, based on the interview, was sent electronically to each participating agency for distribution to their managers and practitioners. A total of 62 completed questionnaires were returned to the research team: 33 from children's social care, 14 from health, 12 from youth offending teams, and 3 from education.

As a result of this two-pronged approach, 147 professionals were able to contribute to the study.

In order to gain a clearer understanding of the organisational context within each agency prior to implementing the Integrated Children's System, the identified link person from health, education, children's social care, police and the youth offending team was interviewed in each participating authority; 20 interviews in total.

THE FIRST AUDIT OF SOCIAL WORK CASE FILES

The aim of the first audit of social work files was to identify what information was held, within children's social care, on vulnerable children and their

Table A.1 The distribution of interviews by service and local authority

	Unitary Authority	Welsh Local Authority	London Borough	Shire County	Total
Health	5	3	7	6	21
Education	4	5	5	4	18
Police	0	1	3	3	7
Children's Social Care	5	6	6	7	24
Youth Justice	2	3	3	7	15
Total	16	18	24	27	85

families, prior to the implementation of the Integrated Children's System. Information was gathered on children's needs, the services they receive from all agencies and the children's developmental progress. Although the focus of the audit was primarily on whether a piece of information had been recorded, for some data items criteria were established to assess the quality of the information recorded. During this audit information was sourced from all records on social work case files.

In order to select the audit sample, each participating local authority provided the research team with a list of all cases open on a designated date and that met the following criteria:

- child with complex needs living at home
- child's name is on the Child Protection Register
- child is looked after
- young person looked after who has a Pathway Plan setting out how they will move into adulthood
- child with disabilities (physical and/or learning disabilities, or emotional and behavioural problems); this group to include cases where the child has complex needs and is living at home, cases where the child is receiving short break care, cases where the child is living in residential care, and cases where the child is in transition to adult services.

To be included in the audit sample more than one agency or organisation had to be involved, and the child and their family had to be receiving different types of intervention for different purposes. The objective was to include, from each authority, 10 cases from each of the first four groups and 12 cases from the last group (two from each sub-category of children with disabilities). This resulted in a total of 150 cases involving 577 records being scrutinised.

The audit of cases prior to the implementation of the Integrated Children's System revealed a number of issues that not only hampered the collection of data but have wider implications for good practice.

1. The amount of recorded material. Children who have a long history of intervention from children's services are likely to generate extensive paperwork. For example, in one case the research team were presented with nine separate volumes. However, in many cases the files were bolstered by duplicated documentation; it was not uncommon to find several copies of the child's review or court reports. Questioning the practitioners suggests that this occurred when duplicates of documents are found to be superfluous; rather than destroying them they were included in the child's file.

2. The order of the case files. Children's case files were generally divided into discrete sections in order to identify more easily key material about the child. However, the study showed this was not always successful; in some files material within a particular section was out of order, or documents were filed in the wrong section.

3. Out of date assessments and plans. It is essential that assessments and plans for all children are kept up to date. Identifying the latest assessments and care plan revealed that in some cases these were not on the child's open case file, but located on closed files. A failure to bring key records forward meant they were rarely reviewed or updated.

4. An absence of key documents. In some cases key documents could not be located on the case files. For example, chronologies were often present in cases involving care proceedings, but otherwise few were found irrespective of the nature and complexity of the case. Without a chronology it was often difficult to determine the sequence of events in a child's history. Similarly, in cases where a child's name had been placed on the child protection register it was often difficult to locate detailed information relating to results of strategy discussions or the outcome of s47 enquiries.

Stage 3: Training staff on the Integrated Children's System
TRAINING SESSIONS

The research team provided each local authority with up to five training or familiarisation days, which they could use as they wished. To ensure consistency the sessions were delivered by a member of the research team who is an experienced trainer. Most of the authorities opted for a mix of multi-agency briefing sessions (up to three in a day) and longer half day or one day training sessions. Training was provided for over 700 staff across the four local authorities.

THE DEVELOPMENT OF A TRAINING AND RESOURCE PACK

It was evident that pilot authorities would require some practical assistance with introducing the Integrated Children's System. Whilst there were champions and enthusiasts about the system in the four pilot authorities, there were not yet the trainers in place within the organisations or available on a consultancy basis who had expertise and experience in the Integrated Children's System. A training pack was, therefore, designed by the research team, drawing on their earlier experiences of implementation and training (see Cleaver *et al.* 2004a; Corrick *et al.* 1995), to support the pilot authorities and their partner agencies in introducing the Integrated Children's System (Walker *et al.* 2003b). It was aimed at inter-agency audiences of practitioners and managers working with children and their families and was intended to be used by trainers in the authorities in three ways to:

- introduce practitioners and managers to the key messages from research, policy and practice which had influenced the development of the Integrated Children's System
- provide opportunities for practitioners and managers to familiarise themselves with the practice materials
- enable them to gain experience in using the practice materials.

It was emphasised that any training on the Integrated Children's System should be co-ordinated with training on IT because IT was a fundamental component of the system. The Training and Resource Pack was structured on a modular basis and provided briefing material on the important issues of implementation and training and on the key practice processes, as well as including training exercises and other materials. In addition, there were cross-references to relevant training materials commissioned earlier by the Department of Health, such as The Child's World: Assessing Children in

Need Training and Development Pack (NSPCC and University of Sheffield 2000), HOME Inventory: A Training Approach for the UK (Cox and Walker 2002) and the Write Enough Training Materials (Walker *et al.* 2003a). Each participating local authority was provided with a copy of the pack.

CONFERENCES

To support the training the research team facilitated five one-day conferences which were open to all relevant agencies and organisations within the four participating authorities. Each authority hosted one conference, the fifth being hosted by the research team. The conferences provided a forum where issues and experiences arising from each authority's implementation and training strategy could be shared and, alongside early findings from the study, used to inform their ongoing implementation process. The conferences were well attended by managers and practitioners from children's social care, health, education, youth justice and the police as well as IT specialists from children's social care. In addition, representatives from the then Department for Education and Skills (now the Department for Children, Schools and Families) and the Welsh Assembly Government attended and updated the authorities on policy initiatives related to the Integrated Children's System. A series of Briefing Papers were commissioned by the Department for Education and Skills to bring together the early messages from the project. These were available to the pilot sites through the Integrated Children's System website (www.everychildmatters.gov.uk/socialcare/integratedchildrenssystem/briefingpapers).

Stage 4: Gathering follow-up data

In order to gather any meaningful information on the impact of the Integrated Children's System on practice, local authorities had to have been using the system for at least six months.

UTILISING SETBACKS TO THE RESEARCH TIMETABLE

All four local authorities experienced set-backs and delays to their planned implementation timetable. As a result, and in consultation with the Research Advisory Group, the follow-up aspect of the study was delayed for six months.

An exploration of the reasons for delay showed local authorities could address some issues more easily than others. For example, one authority, having to replace quickly their existing IT system, focused primarily on IT training during the early months of their implementation. Staff training on practice issues required additional time resulting in delays to their implementation schedule. In the other three authorities delays in implementation were directly related to IT; they encountered both developmental and technical issues. When the IT system was developed in-house or in partnership with small providers, difficulties could be more easily addressed. In fact, one authority whose IT development was out of their direct control was unable to implement before the end of the research project. As a result follow-up data could only be gathered from three authorities.

To allow for these delays and for the research team to consider in more detail the challenges faced by organisations planning to implement the Integrated Children's System as a computer-based system, the commissioning agencies agreed to fund the study for an additional six months.

The additional funding and time was used to:

- consider the effectiveness of the different processes used by local authorities to develop their IT models
- identify the most successful approaches used by the authorities in supporting practitioners to use IT.

RESEARCH TOOLS USED TO GATHER INFORMATION

To understand fully the impact of the Integrated Children's System on practice and the development of IT systems, a range of different methods were used. These included:

- a second audit of social work case files
- a series of multi-agency workshops – attendees completed short questionnaires
- questionnaires completed by staff in children's social care
- questionnaires completed by looked after young people
- questionnaires completed by the Integrated Children's System leads and the authority's IT leads
- field trips to the authorities.

A second audit of social work case files

The second audit focused primarily on the information contained within each authority's Integrated Children's System. However, when authorities had used the Integrated Children's System to develop their own version of particular records, such as a core assessment record or a looked after child's review form, these were included in the audit.

The first audit provided information on social work recording prior to the Integrated Children's System. The aim of the second audit was to focus on similar groups of children to those involved in the first audit, and by gathering the same information identify the extent to which the Integrated Children's System had affected practice. This was explored both in terms of what was recorded and to a lesser extent the quality of the recording.

The same methodology was used to select the second audit sample, with the added proviso that key work had been done since the implementation. For example, the group 'whose names are on the Child Protection Register' would have had to have been registered since the introduction of the Integrated Children's System. The second audit sample included 143 cases and involved the scrutiny of 785 records.

A series of multi-agency workshops – attendees completed short questionnaires

Two half day workshops were held in the three authorities that had implemented the Integrated Children's System: one focused on staff within children's social care and the other was open to all partner agencies, i.e. health, education, youth offending teams and the police. The workshops provided an opportunity for emerging findings from the study to be shared and for practitioners and managers to provide insights and comments on the data and the implications for practice for their agency. Seventy-eight professionals attended the workshops.

Prior to any group discussions, attendees completed a questionnaire which explored their experiences of the Integrated Children's System. The questionnaire focused on the impact of the Integrated Children's System on inter-agency practice in terms of information sharing, agency's own recording practice, and inter-agency working relationships.

All 78 professionals completed the questionnaire: 52 from within children's social care, 14 from health, 9 from education, 2 from the police and 1 from housing. The group was fairly equally split between managers and practitioners.

Questionnaires completed by staff in children's social care

A questionnaire was made available to staff in children's social care through the link professional. The focus of the questionnaire was to explore the impact of the Integrated Children's System on social workers' attitudes and use of IT, and on the IT training they received.

A total of 46 professionals within children's social care responded. Although the numbers are small they included practitioners from a broad spectrum of work and responsibilities, including: family placement, leaving care coordination, children with disabilities, initial response and assessment, conference reviewing and coordination, family support, short break care, community services, permanency and quality assurance.

Questionnaires completed by looked after young people

A questionnaire was developed to explore the impact of the Integrated Children's System on the experiences of young people looked after. This covered a number of issues in-depth including young people's involvement and experience of plans, reviews and decision making. The link person working within children's social care in each participating authority agreed to forward a questionnaire to all their young people looked after. This resulted in responses from 34 young people from one authority. Despite considerable encouragement from the research team, no responses were forthcoming from the other authorities. After six months and in consultation with the Research Advisory Group it was decided not to pursue this further.

Questionnaires completed by the Integrated Children's System leads and the authority's IT leads

In order to gather details of the pilot authorities' IT systems and the process through which they were developed, two questionnaires were emailed to the Integrated Children's System project lead and the IT lead in all four participating local authorities.

One questionnaire explored the functionality of the IT system local authorities had to support the Integrated Children's System. For example, information was sought on whether the system provided alerts for key case events such as reviews, statistical data on the activity of a social work team, invitations to relevant professionals for meetings, and alerts and warnings about a child's special needs.

The second questionnaire explored the process through which the authority had developed their IT system. The questions covered the planning process, issues that affected the plan, factors that promoted or hampered the development process, and the extent to which their IT system met their requirements.

Field trips to the authorities

In order to understand the local authority's Integrated Children's System IT system more comprehensively, a member of the research team with specialist IT skills visited each site. The visit was divided into three parts: a meeting with the project lead; with the IT lead; and a demonstration on the authority's IT system.

The purpose of the meetings with the project lead and the IT lead was to explore and expand issues identified in their recently completed questionnaires. In viewing each authority's Integrated Children's System IT system particular attention was given to understanding the following issues:

- user interface
- level of workflow management
- data retention
- data structures
- user levels
- basic case details
- alerts
- reports
- case notes
- guidance/help
- sibling groups
- white space.

A format was designed to ensure information on each feature was recorded systematically.

MANAGING THE DATA

The study included both an exploratory element (describing the strategy used by the four participating authorities to implement the Integrated Children's System including the IT system to support it) and an evaluative element (assessing its impact on direct work with children, information sharing and inter-agency work, and planning and performance management). The study gathered data at two points in time using a variety of methods, including:

- a scrutiny of policies, procedures and recording formats used before implementation by education, health, youth offending teams and the police
- an audit of social work case files both before and after implementation
- interviews with service providers, carried out before implementation
- questionnaire surveys involving practitioners and managers in children's social care, health, education, youth offending teams and the police, administered both before and after implementation
- questionnaires for young people looked after, sent only after implementation
- questionnaires and interviews with the Integrated Children's System lead and the IT lead, carried out after implementation
- site visits carried out after implementation.

The data gathered from the various methods of investigation were subjected to both quantitative and qualitative methods of analysis.

The information gathered from examining the documentation (policies, procedures and recording formats) was recorded on a standardised pro-forma to ensure consistency. Qualitative methods were used to identify commonalities and differences between the same documents, for example between the recording formats in terms of what was recorded and the language that was used.

The information gathered from the two case file audits was subjected to quantitative methods of analysis using Statistical Package for Social Sciences (SPSS).

The interviews and questionnaires for service providers included both closed and open questions. The replies to the closed questions were analysed using SPSS and answers to open questions provided illustrative material. When the sample size allowed tests of significance were applied, but when numbers were too small the data were presented in terms of frequency counts.

The 34 young people's questionnaires were treated in a similar way; closed questions were analysed using SPSS and answers to open questions used to provide insights into why things were happening. To understand if young people's experiences had changed, the findings were compared with those from previous research. The other data sources included a survey of 706 children and young people in public care (Timms and Thoburn 2003); interviews with 15 young people about their experiences of reviews (Walker 1999); observations of 42 meetings and reviews for children looked after (Grimshaw and Sinclair 1997); and interviews with 116 young people looked after (Triseliotis *et al.* 1995).

The number of questionnaires and interviews with Integrated Children's System leads and IT leads (n=8) and the number of site visits (n=4) meant the data could not be subjected to any sophisticated statistical analysis. Qualitative methods were used to identify differences and similarities in the functionality of the Integrated Children's System IT systems introduced by the four local authorities. Finally, to explore how far the systems met operational needs, the statement of business requirements for the Integrated Children's System issued by the Department for Education and Skills was used as a benchmark.

Summary points

- The study explores the extent to which the Integrated Children's System provides the foundation for achieving better outcomes for children. To do this it identifies its impact on the following issues: direct work with children and families, inter-agency working and information sharing, individual and strategic planning, performance management, and IT systems.

- The study had four distinct stages:
  - selection of four local authorities
  - gathering base-line data
  - provision of training on the Integrated Children's System
  - gathering follow-up data at least six months after authorities had implemented the Integrated Children's System.

- Four local authorities (three English and one Welsh) were selected from 28 applicants to participate in the study. A shortlist of nine authorities was drawn up based on material submitted by the authorities. Each was visited to gather additional information. Anonymised reports were produced from which the final selection of four authorities was made.

- Base-line information was gathered using a range of methods including an audit of social work case files, a scrutiny of blank recording formats used by agencies other than children's social care, and interviews and questionnaires with service providers from all the participating agencies.

- Five training or familiarisation days were provided by the research team. Over 700 professionals from the four authorities were involved. The research team developed a Training and Resource Pack which was provided to each authority to support their continuing training programme. In addition five one-day conferences for the participating authorities were facilitated by the team to support their implementation process.

- All four local authorities experienced set-backs and delays to their planned implementation timetable. To accommodate this, the research was extended by six months. The additional time was used by the study team to explore the IT used to support the implementation of the Integrated Children's System.

- Only three local authorities were able to participate in the follow-up study, one not having managed to implement the Integrated Children's System in time. A range of methods were again used to gather information on its impact. The methods included: a second audit of social work case files; multi-agency workshops where attendees completed short questionnaires; questionnaires completed by staff in children's social care, looked after young people, and each authority's lead for their Integrated Children's System and their IT system; and field trips involving a demonstration of the authority's Integrated Children's System IT system.

- The data were subjected to both quantitative and qualitative methods of analysis. Qualitative methods were used to identify commonalities and differences between the blank recording formats, and to explore the functionality of the Integrated Children's System IT systems introduced by the four local authorities. The interviews and questionnaires for service providers and the findings from the young people's questionnaires included both closed and open questions; the replies to the closed questions were analysed using the computer statistical package SPSS, and answers to open questions provided illustrative material. The information gathered from the audit of social work case files was analysed using SPSS.

References

A National Voice (1999) *Response to Me, Survive Out There? The Report on the Findings of a Young People's Consultation Conference.* London: A National Voice.

Adoption and Children Act 2002. London: The Stationery Office.

Aldgate, J. and Statham, J. (2001) *The Children Act Now: Messages from Research.* London: The Stationery Office.

Armstrong, H. (1997) *Refocusing Children's Services.* Conference, 26 September 1996. London: Department of Health.

Birchall, E. and Hallett, C. (1995) *Working Together in Child Protection.* London: HMSO.

Brandon, M., Howe, A., Dagley, V., Salter, C., Warren, C. and Black, J. (2006) *Evaluating the Common Assessment Framework and Lead Professional Guidance and Implementation in 2005–6,* DfES Research Report, 740. Nottingham: Department for Education and Skills.

Brookes, I. and Bates, P. (1994) 'The problems of effecting change in the british civil service a cultural perspective.' *British Journal of Management 5,* 3, 177–90.

Buchanan, D. and Boddy, D. (1995) *The Expertise of the Change Agent. Public Performance and Backstage Activity.* New York: Prentice Hall.

Cabinet Office (2000) *E-Government: A Strategic Framework for Public Services in the Information Age.* London: Cabinet Office.

Children Act 1989. London: The Stationery Office.

Children Act 2004. London: The Stationery Office.

Children (Leaving Care) Act 2000. London: The Stationery Office.

Children and Young People's Unit (2001) *Building a Strategy for Children and Young People: A Consultation Document.* London: Children and Young People's Unit.

Cleaver, H. (1996) *Focus on Teenagers: Research into Practice.* London: HMSO.

Cleaver, H. (2004) *Fostering Family Contact.* London: The Stationery Office.

Cleaver, H. and Freeman, P. (1995) *Parental Perspectives in Cases of Suspected Child Abuse.* London: HMSO.

Cleaver, H. and Nicholson, D. (2005) *The Development and Use of a Local Prototype Common Referral, Information and Assessment Record in Cumbria.* Cumbria: Cumbria Children's Fund.

Cleaver, H., Unell, I. and Aldgate, J. (1999) *Children's Needs – Parenting Capacity: The Impact of Parental Mental Illness, Problem Alcohol and Drug Use, and Domestic Violence on Children's Development.* London: The Stationery Office.

Cleaver, H., Barnes, J., Bliss, D. and Cleaver, D. (2004a) *Developing Information Sharing and Assessment Systems.* Research Report 597. London: Department for Education and Skills.

Cleaver, H. and Walker, S. with Meadows, P. (2004b) *Assessing Children's Needs and Circumstances.* London: Jessica Kingsley Publishers.

Cleaver, H., Nicholson, D., Tarr, S. and Cleaver, D. (2007) *Child Protection, Domestic Violence and Parental Substance Misuse: Family Experiences and Effective Practice.* London: Jessica Kingsley Publishers.

Cm 4776 (2000) *Learning the Lessons. The Government's Response to Lost in Care: The Report of the Tribunal of Inquiry into the Abuse of Children in Care in the Former County Council Areas of Gwynedd and Clwyd since 1974.* London: The Stationery Office.

Cm 5730 (2003) *The Victoria Climbié Inquiry.* London: The Stationery Office.

Cm 5860 (2003) *Every Child Matters.* London: The Stationery Office.

Cm 5861 (2003) *Keeping Children Safe: The Government's Response to the Victoria Climbié Inquiry Report and Joint Chief Inspectors' Report Safeguarding Children.* London: The Stationery Office.

Cm 6932 (2006) *Care Matters: Transforming the Lives of Children and Young People in Care.* London: The Stationery Office.

Codd, E.F. (1970) 'A Relational Model of Data for Large Shared Data Banks.' *Communications of ACM, 13,* 6, 377–87.

Connors, C. and Stalker, K. (2005) 'Better than Being at Home: Disabled Children's Views about School.' In J. Scott and H. Ward (eds) *Promoting and Safeguarding the Well-being of Children, Families and Communities.* London: Jessica Kingsley Publishers.

Corner, A., Rushforth, C. and Shemmings, D. (1999) 'Preparing Children for Involvement in Decision-making.' In D. Shemmings (ed.) *Involving Children in Family Support and Child Protection.* London: The Stationery Office.

Corrick, H., Jones, D. and Ward, H. (1995) *Looking After Children: Management and Implementation Guide.* London: HMSO.

Cox, A. and Walker, S. (2002) *The HOME Inventory: A Training Approach for the UK.* Brighton: Pavilion Publishers.

Data Protection Act 1998 (1998) London: The Stationery Office.

Department for Education and Skills (2003a) *Core Information Requirements.* Accessed on 10/10/07 at www.everychildmatters.gov.uk/search/IG00009/

Department for Education and Skills (2003b) *e-Record Demonstrator.* Published on CD. London: Department for Education and Skills.

Department for Education and Skills (2003c) *Children's Social Services Core Information Requirements. Data Model Version 3.1.* London: Department of Health. Accessed on 07/05/08 at www.everychildmatters.gov.uk/resources-and-practice/IG00009

Department for Education and Skills (2003d) *Children's Social Services Core Information Requirements. Process Model Version 3.1.* London: Department of Health. Accessed on 07/05/08 at www.everychildmatters.gov.uk/resources-and-practice/IG00009

Department for Education and Skills (2004) *IT for ICS: A Guidance Note on Functionality for RDWs: v4.0 (December 2004).* London: Department for Education and Skills.

Department for Education and Skills (2005a) *Integrated Children's System: A Statement of Business Requirements.* Children's Social Services Local Authority Circular LAC(2005)3. London: Department for Education and Skills. Accessed on 10/10/07 at www.everychild matters.gov.uk/_files/A31CC68380F45993BCE8 BE47845D3C7D.pdf

Department for Education and Skills (2005b) *The Information Technology for the Integrated Children System Investment Strategy. Frequently Asked Questions (Version 1.0).* London: Department for Education and Skills.

Department for Education and Skills (2006a) Letter to Chief Executives 26 May 2006, from Althea Efunshile, Director, Safeguarding Children Group, Integrated Children's System (ICS) Delivery. London: Department for Children, Schools and Families.

Department for Education and Skills (2006b) *About the Integrated Children's System.* London: Department for Education and Skills. Accessed on 10/10/07 at www.everychildmatters.gov.uk/resources-and-practice/IG00009

Department for Education and Skills (2007) *The Integrated Children's System: Minimum Compliance Criteria.* London: Department of Education and Skills. Accessed on 10/10/07 at www.everychildmatters.gov.uk/resources-and-practice/IG00189

Department for the Environment, Transport and the Regions (2000) *Indices of Deprivation.* Accessed on 10/10/07 at http://www.statistics.gov.uk/StatBase/Product.asp?vlnk= 9421&Pas= 1&ColRank= 2&Rank=272

Department of Health (1989) *Quality Protects: Framework for Action.* London: Department of Health.

Department of Health (1991) *The Children Act 1989 Guidance and Regulations, Volume 3: Family Placements.* London: HMSO.

Department of Health (1995a) *Looking After Children: Good Parenting, Good Outcomes.* London: The Stationery Office.

Department of Health (1995b) *Child Protection: Messages from Research.* London: HMSO.

Department of Health (1995c) *Looking After Children Materials: Essential Information Records, Plans, Reviews, Consultation Papers and Assessment and Action Records.* London: HMSO.

Department of Health (1999) *The Government's Objectives for Children's Social Services.* London: Department of Health.

Department of Health (2000) *Assessing Children in Need: Practice Guidance.* London: The Stationery Office.

Department of Health (2001a) *Children (Leaving Care) Act 2000: Regulations and Guidance.* London: Department of Health.

Department of Health (2001b) *Children's Social Services Core Information Requirements: Executive Summary (Version 2. July 2001).* London: Department of Health. Accessed on 10/10/07 at www.everychildmatters.gov.uk/resources-and-practice/IG00009

Department of Health (2002a) *Promoting the Health of Looked After Children.* London: The Stationery Office.

Department of Health (2002b) *Integrated Children's System: Working with Children in Need and their Families – Consultation Document.* London: Department of Health. Accessed on 10/10/07 at www.everychildmatters.gov.uk/socialcare

Department of Health (2006) *Research Governance Framework for Health and Social Care.* London: Department of Health.

Department of Health and Cleaver, H. (2000) *Framework for the Assessment of Children in Need and their Families: Assessment Recording Forms.* London: The Stationery Office.

Department of Health and Department for Education and Skills (2000–2005) *Integrated Children's System Briefing Papers 1–8.* Accessed on 07/05/08 at www.everychildmatters.gov.uk/ resources-and-practice/IG00009

Department of Health and Department for Education and Skills (2004) *National Service Framework for Children, Young People and Maternity Services.* London: The Stationery Office.

Department of Health and the Welsh Assembly Government (2002) *Integrated Children's System Working with Children in Need and their Families: Consultation Draft.* London: Department of Health.

Department of Health, Home Office and Department for Education and Employment (1999) *Working Together to Safeguard Children: A Guide to Inter-agency Working to Safeguard and Promote the Welfare of Children.* London: The Stationery Office.

Department of Health, Department for Education and Employment, and Home Office (2000a) *Framework for the Assessment of Children in Need and their Families.* London: The Stationery Office.

Department of Health, Cox, A. and Bentovim, A. (2000b) *The Family Assessment Pact of Questionnaires and Scales.* London: The Stationery Office.

Docherty, T. and Horne, T. (2002) *Managing Public Services: Implementing Changes – A Thoughtful Approach.* London: Routledge.

Dunn, J. and McGuire, S. (1992) 'Sibling and peer relationships in childhood.' *Journal of Child Psychology and Psychiatry 33,* 1, 67–105.

Fletcher, B. (1993) *Not Just a Name: The Views of Young People in Foster and Residential Care.* London: National Consumer Council and Who Cares? Trust.

Gatehouse, M. and Ward, H. (2003) *Making Use of Information in Children's Social Services.* Final Report of the Data Analysis Network for Children's Services Project. Loughborough: Centre for Child and Family Research, Loughborough University.

Gatehouse, M., Statham, J. and Ward, H. (2004a) *Information Outputs for Children's Social Services, (Version 1.0a, February 2004).* Loughborough: Centre for Child and Family Research. Accessed on 10/10/07 at www.everychildmatters.gov.uk/_files/7597AB95 02E9333008105AAAC03 D0FEA.pdf

Gatehouse, M., Statham, J., and Ward, H. (2004b) *The Knowledge: How to Get the Information You Need out of Your Computers and Information Systems. A Practical Guide for Children's Social Services.* Understanding Children's Social Care Series No.9. London: Thomas: Coram Research Unit, Institute of Education. Accessed on 10/10/07 at www.everychildmatters.gov.uk/_files/ 26E4952ED7F925BE1BAF7B12D97A7552.pdf

Grimshaw, R. and Sinclair, R. (1997) *Planning to Care: Regulation, Procedures and Practice under the Children Act 1989.* London: National Children's Bureau.

Gupta, A. and Blewett, J. (2007) 'Change for children? The challenges and opportunities for the children's social work workforce.' *Child and Family Social Work 12,* 2, 172–181.

Handy, C. (1995) *Gods of Management: The Changing Work of Organisations.* London: Arrow Books.

HC 653 (2004) *Bichard Inquiry Report.* London: The Stationery Office.

HM Government (2005a) *Common Core: Skills and Knowledge for the Children's Workforce.* London: Department for Education and Skills.

HM Government (2005b) *Children's Workforce Strategy: A Strategy to Build a World-class Workforce for Children and Young People.* London: Department for Education and Skills.

HM Government (2005c) *Statutory Guidance on Making Arrangements to Safeguard and Promote the Welfare of Children under Section 11 of the Children Act 2004.* London: Department for Education and Skills.

HM Government (2006a) *Care Matters: Transforming the Lives of Children and Young People in Care.* London: The Stationery Office.

HM Government (2006b) *The Common Assessment Framework for Children and Young People: Practitioners' Guide* London: Department for Education and Skills. Accessed on 07/05/08 at www.everychildmatters.gov.uk/ search

HM Government (2006c) *Working Together to Safeguard Children: A Guide to Inter-agency Working to Safeguard and Promote the Welfare of Children*. London: The Stationery Office.

HM Government (2006d) *Information Sharing: Practitioners' Guide. Integrated Working to Improve Outcomes for Children and Young People*. London: Department for Education and Skills.

HM Government (2006e) *What To Do if You're Worried a Child is Being Abused*. London: The Stationery Office.

HM Government (2007) *PSA Delivery Agreement 13: Improve Children and Young People's Safety*. Norwich: HMSO. Accessed on 10/10/07 at www.hm-treasury.gov.uk/ media/8/7/ pbr_csr07_ psa13.pdf

Hudson, B. (2005) 'Will reforms suit users?' *Community Care*, 28 July–3 August, 30–31.

Inter-Agency Group (2004) *From Vision to Reality: Transforming Outcomes for Children and Families*. London: Local Government Association Publications.

Jones, D.P.H (2003) *Communicating with Vulnerable Children: A Guide for Practitioners*. London: Gaskell.

Jones, D.P.H. and Ramchandani, P. (1999) *Child Sexual Abuse: Informing Practice from Research*. Oxon: Radcliffe Medical Press.

Jones, H., Clark, R., Kufeldt, K. and Norman, M. (1998) 'Looking after children: Assessing outcomes in child care: the experience of implementation.' *Children & Society 12*, 212–22.

Jowell, R. (2003) *Trying It Out: The Role of 'Pilots' in Policy-Making. Report on Behalf of the Cabinet Office*. London: The Cabinet Office Strategy Unit.

Kagle, J. D. (1993) 'Record keeping for the 1990s.' *Social Work 38*: 190–196.

Kellmer Pringle, M. and Naidoo, S. (1975) *Early Child Care in Britain*. London: Gordon and Breach.

Kroll, B. and Taylor, A. (2003) *Parental Substance Misuse and Child Welfare*. London: Jessica Kingsley Publishers.

LAC (2002)19 *The Quality Protects Programme: Transforming Children's Services 2003–04*. London: Department of Health.

McConkey, D. (1993) 'Organisational Development in the Public Sector.' In T. Cummings and C. Worley (eds) *Organisational Development and Change*. Michigan: West Publishing Company.

Marchant, R. (2001) 'The Assessment of Children with Complex Needs.' In J. Horwath (ed.) *The Child's World: Assessing Children in Need*. London: Jessica Kingsley Publishers.

Marsh, P. and Peel, M. (1999) *Leaving Care in Partnership: Family Involvement with Care Leavers*. London: The Stationery Office.

Morgan, R. (2007) *Your Right! Your Say: Looked After in England. A Report by the Children's Rights Director for England*. London: Ofsted.

Morris, J. (1998) *Still Missing? The Experience of Disabled Children and Young People Living Away From Home*. London: Who Cares? Trust.

Moyers, S. (1997) *Report of an Audit of the Implementation of Looking After Children in Year 1: 1995/6*. Leicester: University of Leicester.

Murphy, M. and Oulds, G. (2000) 'Establishing and Developing Co-operative Links between Substance Misuse and Child Protection Systems.' In F. Harbin and M. Murphy (eds) *Substance Misuse and Child Care*. Dorset: Russell House Publishing.

National Assembly for Wales (2000a) *Working Together to Safeguard Children: A Guide to Inter-agency Working to Safeguard and Promote the Welfare of Children*. London: The Stationery Office.

National Assembly for Wales (2000b) *Children and Young People: A Framework for Partnership*. Cardiff: National Assembly for Wales.

National Assembly for Wales (2001a) *Guidance on the Education of Children Looked After by Local Authorities, Circular 2/2001 and Guidance*. Cardiff: National Assembly for Wales.

National Assembly for Wales (2001b) *Framework for the Assessment of Children in Need and their Families*. London: The Stationery Office.

National Assembly for Wales (2005) *National Service Framework for Children, Young People and Maternity Services in Wales*. Cardiff: Welsh Assembly Government.

National Assembly for Wales (2006) *Towards a Stable Life and a Brighter Future*. Cardiff: National Assembly for Wales. Accessed on 10/10/07 at http://new.wales.gov.uk/ topics/childrenyoungpeople/childrenfirst/ lookedafterchildren/regulationsguidancelookedafter?lang=en

NSPCC and University of Sheffield (2000) *The Child's World: Assessing Children in Need Training and Developmetn Pack*. Leicester: NSPCC.

Parker, R.A., Ward, H., Jackson, S., Aldgate, J. and Wedge, P. (eds) (1991) *Looking After Children: Assessing Outcomes in Child Care*. London: HMSO.

Peel, M. (1998) *Report of an Audit of the Implementation of Looking After Children in Year 2: 1996/7*. Leicester: University of Leicester.

Performance and Innovation Unit (2000) *Adding It Up: Improving Analysis and Modelling in Central Government.* London: Cabinet Office.

Reder, P. and Duncan, S. (2003) 'How Much Should Children's Views Count.' In P. Reder, P, S. Duncan and C. Lucey (eds) *Studies in the Assessment of Parenting.* Hove: Brunner-Routledge.

Rose, W., Aldgate, J. and Barnes, J. (2007) 'From Policy Visions to Practice Realities: The Pivotal Role of Service Managers in Implementation.' In J. Aldgate, L. Healy, B. Malcolm, B.E. Pine, W. Rose, and J. Seden (eds) *Enhancing Social Work Management: Theory and best Practice from the UK and the USA.* London: Jessica Kingsley Publishers.

Rutter, M. (1985) 'Resilience in the face of adversity: protective factors and resistance to psychiatric disorder.' *British Journal of Psychiatry 47,* 598–611.

Scott, J. (1999) *Report of an Audit of the Implementation of Looking After Children in Year 2: 1997/8.* Leicester: University of Leicester.

Scott, J. (2000) *Report of a Longitudinal Audit of the Implementation of Looking After Children by Local Authorities which Implemented Looking After Children in Year 1: 1995/6.* Leicester: University of Leicester.

Social Exclusion Unit (2003) *A better Education for Children in Care.* London: Social Exclusion Unit, Office of the Deputy Prime Minister.

Social Services Inspectorate (1997) *Responding to Families in Need: Inspection of Assessment, Planning and Decision-Making in Family Support Services.* London: Department of Health.

Social Services Inspectorate (1998) *Social Services Facing the Future: The Seventh Annual Report of the Chief Inspector, Social Services Inspectorate, 1997/98.* London: The Stationery Office.

Social Services Inspectorate (1999) *Recording With Care: Inspection of Case Recording in Social Services Departments.* London: Department of Health.

Stein, M. (2004) *What Works for Young People Leaving Care?* Barkingside: Barnardo's.

Thomas, N. and O'Kane, C. (1998) 'When children's wishes and feelings clash with their "best interests".' *International Journal of Children's Rights 6,* 2, 137–54.

Timms, J.E. and Thoburn, J. (2003) *Your Shout! A Survey of the Views of 706 Children and Young People in Public Care.* London: NSPCC.

Triseliotis, J., Borland, M., Hill, M. and Lambert, L. (1995) *Teenagers and the Social Work Services.* London: HMSO.

United Nations (1989) *Convention on the Rights of the Child.* Accessed on 10/10/07 at www.unhchr.ch/html/menu3/b/k2crc.htm

Walker, S. (1999) 'Children's Perspectives on Attending Statutory Reviews.' In D. Shemmings (ed.) *Involving Children in Family Support and Child Protection.* London: The Stationery Office.

Walker, S., Shemmings, D. and Cleaver, H. (2003a) *Write Enough: Effective Recording in Children's Services.* CD ROM. Accessed on 10/10/07 at http://www.writeenough.org.uk

Walker, S., Scott, J. and Cleaver, H. (2003b) *Using the Integrated Children's System: A Training and Resource Pack.* London: Department of Health. Accessed on 10/10/07 at www.everychildmatters.gov.uk/search/IG00024

Ward, H. (ed.) (1995a) *Looking After Children: Research into Practice.* London: HMSO.

Ward, H. (1995b) 'Research Messages for Implementation.' In H. Ward (ed.) *Looking After Children: Research into Practice.* London: HMSO.

Ward, H., Skuse, T. and Munro, E. (2005) 'The best of times, the worst of times: young people's views of care and accommodation.' *Adoption and Fostering 29,*1,8–17.

Welsh Assembly Government (2004) *Children and Young People: Rights to Action.* Cardiff: Welsh Assembly Government.

Welsh Assembly Government (2005a) *Care Leavers Survey: Overall Summary.* Cardiff: Welsh Assembly Government.

Welsh Assembly Government (2005b) *Integrated Children's System: A Statement of Business Requirements, Circular 21/2005.* Cardiff: Welsh Assembly Government. Accessed on 10/10/07 at http://ssia.wlga.gov.uk/index.cfm?articleid=1587

Welsh Assembly Government (2006) *The Wales Accord for the Sharing of Personal Information.* Accessed on 07/05/08 at: www.nhs.uk/site3/home.cfm?orgid=702

Welsh Index of Multiple Deprivation (2000) Accessed on 10/10/07 at www.statistics.gov.uk/ StatBase/Product.asp?vlnk=9421&Pas=1&ColRank=2&Rank=272

Welsh Office (1999) *The Children First Programme in Wales: Transforming Children's Services, Welsh Office Circular 20/99.* Cardiff: National Assembly for Wales.

Subject Index

Author Index